# Päntsdrunk

# Päntsdrunk

## (*Kalsarikänni*)

## THE FINNISH PATH TO RELAXATION

### (Drinking at Home, Alone, in Your Underwear)

**Miska Rantanen**

HARPER
DESIGN
*An Imprint of HarperCollinsPublishers*

Published by agreement with Helsinki Literary Agency, Helsinki, Finland. Originally published under the title *Kalsarikänni: suomalainen opas hyvään elämään* by Kustantamo S&S, in 2018.

Pantsdrunk

Published in 2018 by

Harper Design
*An Imprint of* HarperCollins*Publishers*
195 Broadway
New York, NY 10007
Tel: (212) 207-7000
Fax: (855) 746-6023
harperdesign@harpercollins.com
www.hc.com

Distributed throughout the world by
HarperCollins Publishers
195 Broadway
New York, NY 10007

ISBN 978-0-06-285589-3

Library of Congress Cataloging-in-Publication Data has been applied for.

Printed in the United States of America

First Printing, 2018

*For Stella, Jallu and Santtu*

# Contents

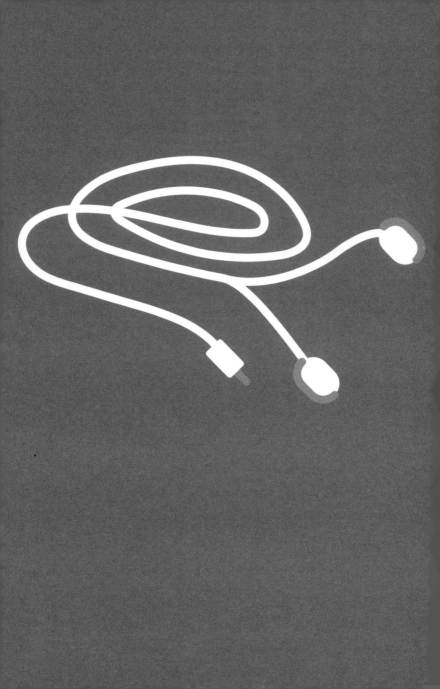

# Prologue

*Sound familiar?*

It's been a long day, one meeting after another. Despite the idiocy of most of your clients, you've maintained a poker face worthy of an Oscar. There's been no end to the surprising situations and quick-fire decisions, and your brain is in overdrive.

You walk in the door and realize to your relief that you've done all you can for now. You've earned the right to be pleased with yourself.

Now, you could head out to the bars with your contacts; maybe network until the wee hours. A couple of drinks would definitely hit the spot. But you decide to call it a night and stay in.

The reason? You've had the foresight to prepare.

That morning you packed the fridge full of budget-brand artisanal beer from the corner store. A mini-bottle of champagne, another of hard liquor, and some sweet and salty snacks also made their way into your shopping basket.

During the day, tempers ran hot, but now the beer's cold. You strip off your outer layers of clothing. The basic rule: any article that's appropriate and attractive is also constricting and uncomfortable. In the end, you reach the most pleasurable moment of your striptease: the slow peeling of sweaty socks from your feet, a sensation deserving of its own expression. You fling your them victoriously across the room—and you're free from the shackles of civilization!

You plop down on the couch in your underwear and let out a deep sigh of relief, but the best is yet to come.

You mosey to the fridge and whip out a cold one. The bottle starts to sweat the instant it hits room temperature. As always, bottle opener, bottle cap, and muscle power work in seamless synergy: *zzzhhhh*.

You grab the remote, gallop through the respectable channels—now is not the time for news about market fluctuations in the price of gold. When you start hitting the reality shows (or what can conceivably be interpreted as such), you pump the brakes and take your first swig of beer. Then another. You grab a second cold one to replace the one you just downed and pour yourself a

finger and a half of whisky while you're at it. You crack a bag of chips as tenderly as an ancient treasure chest.

Gradually the tension melts from your shoulders and the warmth slides down to your fingertips. You curl up into a more comfortable position on the couch.

On television, a lifestyle guru proclaims that the color for this fall is burnt orange. Click. On the next channel, young adults who have lost every last shred of personal dignity mate for money on a tropical island. Click. The unsteady camera on the third channel proves it's possible to tune your vehicle for DIY prices: you can find great deals on new suspensions online.

The ride-pimper on TV is working against deadline, but you're not in a hurry to get anywhere. Not anymore.

It's time to get pantsdrunk.

# 1
# Zen,
# the Finnish Way

*What is pantsdrunk? What's the underlying philosophy? How does it differ from* lagom *and* hygge?

Pantsdrunk is R&R for a restless world. If we believe the husky-sized headlines barking at us every which way we turn, the end is nigh. It's almost impossible to tell what's real news, fake news, or both. Climate change, international terrorism, Auto-Tune pop, democratically elected presidents, the plastic surgery of aging celebrities— each bit of news is more depressing than the last.

The Nordic countries have a range of traditional antidotes to weltschmerz. When the storms of the world

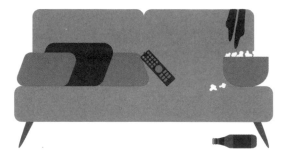

rage, peace-loving Scandinavians know there's little the individual can do to have an appreciable impact. What you can do is concentrate on yourself and your loved ones in hopes of making things easier—or at least slightly more tolerable.

In Sweden and Norway, this philosophy is emblematized by the concept of *lagom*, which is both a saying and a precept. *Lagom* can be translated as "in moderation," "in perfect balance," or "just right." Where *lagom* reigns, all is as it should be. Proportion is maintained: there's neither too much nor too little. *Lagom* is democratic, ecological, and in many respects the true essence of Nordic thinking.

Which is where the problem lies. Although *lagom* encapsulates nearly all aspects of the well-lived life, its puritanism isn't compatible with the realities of the

2010s. The modern human may be responsible, but he or she is also an individualist who wants to make decisions freely, find relief from daily trials and tribulations, and get silly sometimes. The problem with *lagom* lies in its emphasis on being a good person: a good person can never really kick back, because they're constantly weighing the ethical consequences of their decisions.

Dullness is safe, but so is death.

Denmark, for its part, is renowned for its *hygge*: embracing ambiance, luxuriating in leisureliness, and relishing the moment. *Hygge* is a mug of hot cocoa in the warm glow of candlelight while snow drifts down outside the window. Whereas *lagom* is a state of mind and an attitude toward life, *hygge* is achieved by constructing and shaping your physical environment. And it's true: you'd have to be emotionally dead to be immune to the gratifying anesthesia of a wool blanket, a blazing fire, some organic Brie, a supple red wine, and a row of leather-bound spines on the bookshelf.

*Hygge* is the glossy image we've all seen on the pages of interior design magazines and lifestyle blogs. And this is its failing: not all of us have the means to lie by a brick fireplace burning birch logs on stormy autumn evenings. *Hygge* is like a Disney movie that leaves no

place for hemorrhoids, mucusy tears of self-pity, or questionable stains in any number of locations. It leaves no place for real life.

In the Nordic palette of survival strategies, the Finn relies not on *lagom* or *hygge* but on *kalsarikänni*: the primeval yet surprisingly cosmopolitan concept of "pantsdrunk." It can be adapted to every corner of the world, regardless of circumstance, milieu, or mood.

Pantsdrunk doesn't demand over-the-top arrangements. Affordability and democracy are its hallmarks. It's quick acting and suitable for all who have reached the age of majority.

Pantsdrunk provides an opportunity for authentic, total, and true relaxation.

Pantsdrunk is a fast, effective way of recovering from everyday stress.

Pantsdrunk is the antithesis of posing, performing,

or pretense: one does not post atmospheric images on Instagram while pantsdrunk.

Pantsdrunk is *real*.

The relaxing effect of pantsdrunk derives from simple elements: comfortable clothes, alcohol imbibed in appropriate amounts, and a little something to do. And yet the optimization of these elements is not sufficient on its own. Properly understood, *kalsarikänni* requires openness of mind and a willingness to go with the flow. As a matter of fact, the psycho-emotional aspects of pantsdrunk are akin to mindfulness, where, harnessing skills in awareness, presence, and observation, practitioners focus on experiencing the moment with full acceptance. But where mindfulness guides propose a variety of breathing regimes, pantsdrunk taps physical substances to open up a shortcut to the destination: utter relaxation.

## Reflections on pantsdrunk

"*I discovered pantsdrunk for the first time in my twenties, when life was pretty hectic on just about every front. I was living with roommates at the time, and we'd occasionally engage in group pantsdrunk: throw on some grubby sweats and sip away watching reality TV or some other garbage. More than once, those relaxing evenings ended up in frantic mobilization of our makeup arsenals at the kitchen table, the front door slamming behind us as we teetered to the nearest club an hour before last call. Those were the days! Now, as a working mom, I relish the moments when the family's asleep and I can collapse on the couch with a big glass of red wine and binge-watch a good series from some online service. A well-constructed yet subdued pantsdrunk session also helps me fall asleep a lot easier.*"

— **Woman, 42, publisher**

"When I am pantsdrunk, I often browse corporate information online and check out the turnover of different companies. Or else I browse YouTube. The search terms 'ice hockey' and 'eurodance' bring up all sorts of stuff. I never make it through an entire video; I just jump around the list of recommended videos and end up deeper and further from the original topic."

— **Man, 36, locksmith**

# 2
# Introduction:
# Why Pantsdrunk?

*The cultural origins of pantsdrunk. Dimensions of pantsdrunk. Physical exercise.*

So what exactly is pantsdrunk? The Finnish term *kalsarikänni* [kʌl-sʌ-rɪ-kæn-nɪ] is a simple compound word: *kalsari* (underwear) + *känni* (state of inebriation). This pithy idiom crystallizes the essential: at its simplest, pantsdrunk means imbibing alcohol in one's underwear at home without any intention of going out. The term's ingenuity lies in everything it doesn't imply.

The leitmotif of pantsdrunk is meaningful meaninglessness. When you start and end at zero, the tiniest achievement counts as a victory. Winning is easy, losing is hard.

# The Cultural Origins of Pantsdrunk

As a philosophy, pantsdrunk is not in conflict with *lagom* and *hygge*. Au contraire. They all spring from the same Nordic origins and share the same ultimate goals: optimal peace of mind, joie de vivre, comfort, equilibrium, and recuperation as embodied in a snug coziness.

The present form each of these philosophies takes has been shaped by the history, culture, and national character of the originating country. A fruitful analysis of the differences between *lagom*, *hygge*, and *kalsarikänni* begins by investigating the economic history of the Nordic countries, as Denmark, Norway, and Sweden have deeper roots in well-being than Finland does.

Denmark's prosperity can be explained through its early adoption of agricultural and industrial advances. It also stands at the crossroads of numerous trade routes, which has boosted its economy for centuries. In contrast, Sweden accumulated wealth in the Middle Ages thanks to its ore reserves and in the post-industrial era from flatpacked furniture. Sweden has also established cultural supremacy on the pop music front through the Eurovision contest and an unprofitable streaming service. Norway was known primarily for its cod and herring until the 1960s, when it decided to drill holes in the ocean floor. Since then, Norway has profited from oil reserves so vast that any talk of *lagom*-like moderation is ridiculous.

BLESSED BY A LACK OF NATURAL RESOURCES, Finland was long an agrarian society. Hardscrabble farms dotted the sparsely inhabited landscape at distances of dozens of miles; once they moved to cities, Finns avoided one another out of habit. The primary exports were tar

and butter. In the 1850s, wood and forestry products conquered the export markets. More recently, Finnish industrial output has been complemented by heavy machinery, oil refining, and electronics in the form of mobile phones, Darude's EDM hit "Sandstorm," and Angry Birds.

The spiritual-psychological roots of pantsdrunk are easy to understand when you cast your gaze out the window on a Finnish November day. It's pitch dark and freezing, a lacerating sleet blows horizontally, the ground is crusted in ice and slush, the streets are deserted, and human companionship requires a lengthy and unpleasant trek. And that's at noon, the brightest moment of the day.

Pantsdrunk was doubtless developed during these somber, precipitation-heavy, mirthless seasons, when leaving the house is an insurmountable hurdle. In Finland, that means about nine and a half months of the year.

As a product of Finnish culture, pantsdrunk is a refined form of another Finnish concept: *sisu*, or "grit." At its best, *sisu* means tenacity or perseverance, perhaps even bullheadedness. And yet *sisu* has its dark side. No one has the energy to drain swamps or chase clients 24/7 without a break. When abused, *sisu* has a tendency to burn out those who gullibly swallow earlier generations' exaggerated stories of how they heroically built a house, earned degree after degree, and raised a brood of children while chasing off wolves and kicking the Red Army's butt during the Winter War.

Pantsdrunk is merciful; it doesn't encourage overextension or exhaustion. It revivifies.

Perpetual gloom, freezing temperatures, and long distances demonstrate why pantsdrunk originated and developed in Finnish surroundings. How else could you stand life there? It's best to avoid recounting to a Finn in overly great detail the conditions under which people live in, say, southern Germany: within a few hours' drive, you have the

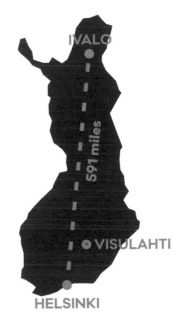

Mediterranean, the Alps, or the vineyards of the Moselle valley. In the same amount of time, a Finn has made it halfway to the neighboring town.

Naturally, Nordic conceptions of gender equality have come to infuse the theory and practice of pantsdrunk. Despite the fact that Finland still has a way to go in achieving equal pay for equal work, tippling on the couch is a fundamental right of every gender identity, whether that be man, woman, both, neither, or computer nerd.

And while advances in gender equality have increased Finnish women's sociopolitical power, they have also exposed a dark side of the business world. When one has to choose between career and family, the choice ultimately ends up in the hands of the company's majority owners. But as we will come to discover, pantsdrunk offers tools for approaching these problematics as well.

# Dimensions of Pantsdrunk

Pantsdrunk aims at total relaxation and presence. It arrests work-induced pressure and irritation through a combination of fermentation-produced alcohol, selective social contact, and norm-free attire. It is the little person's justifiable, environmentally harmless way of cherry-picking the best of what life has to offer.

Pantsdrunk entails an evening spent in a planned fashion without the pressure to accomplish anything. On the surface, this sounds counterintuitive, but it contains profound wisdom. Pantsdrunk is the courage to project your emotions and readiness to live in the moment regardless of your mood. When work-related stress threatens to crush the oxygen out of your lungs, pantsdrunk takes what life has to offer and refines it into quality time. Pantsdrunk allows you to recuperate emotionally, psychologically, and physically when life's strains are twisting you into knots.

Pantsdrunk is a precision strike into free time. It is also a free-time precision strike.

At its most minimal, pantsdrunk is a device for balancing life and work. It can, however, be expanded into a lifestyle and worldview. The beauty of pantsdrunk lies in its possibilities.

Where there's pantsdrunk, there's potential. For instance, a tentatively

begun evening can end raucously, as the limits of a pantsdrunk session are determined solely by its initiator/practitioner. Falling asleep on the couch while watching *Terminator 2* fulfills the fundamental requirements of a pantsdrunk session, but there's nothing to prevent somebody pantsdrunk from ordering a taxi in the middle of the night and heading to a club where the posse is already waiting. But note, in this instance, pantsdrunk has crossed over into partying.

## During What Months Is Pantsdrunk Most Appropriate?

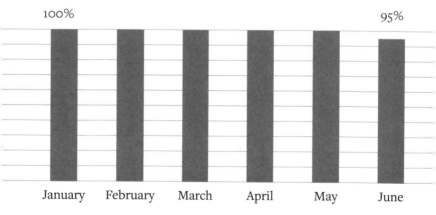

Pantsdrunk can also generate emotional states in which one's capacity for analysis and synthesis seems to overflow. Many professional columnists and authors shamelessly exploit the creativity-inducing effect of pantsdrunk. In contrast, it's best to employ every ounce of restraint to resist filling out government documents.

WHAT SORT OF PHYSICAL EXERCISE is compatible with pantsdrunk? Norra Haga Party Central, an institute

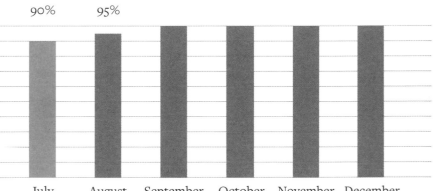

*Source: Norra Haga Party Central*

# How many people are needed for a proper pantsdrunk session?

One: 94%

Two: 3%

Three: 1%

Don't know: 2%

*Source: Norra Haga Party Central*

dedicated to investigating the theory and practice of the Finnish philosophy of pantsdrunk, encourages practitioners to engage in those activities that feel good and generate a sense of joy. Basic movements include stretching, yawning, and shoulder-rolling, but serve primarily to reactivate the motor skills. We recommend boldly crossing that invisible border that separates the formal, the work-oriented, the ceremonial, and the public from your true comfort zone. In this free space, appropriate activities may include spontaneous bathing, belching, intent nose-picking, air guitar-playing, singing, leisurely masturbating, flatulating, talking to yourself, or screaming into a pillow.

PANTSDRUNK DOES NOT NECESSARILY MEAN solo lounging. It can also be done with a good friend, roommate, or perhaps a relative. Pantsdrunk with a friend generally has an empowering effect. Shared inebriation at either end of the couch eases the burden of both individuals, and recharges the batteries regardless of the source of the drain.

When practiced properly, pantsdrunk with one's spouse or significant other expands and deepens the relationship. Getting to know and learn from each other

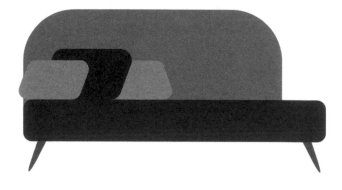

need not take place in a context of sobriety. Closeness is possible even when both parties have a drink within arm's reach and their noses glued to their own screen. Indeed, pantsdrunk can serve to cement the relationship.

This book concentrates on the philosophy and practice of pantsdrunk without extra-inebriatory agendas. By definition, so-called confessional moments are not consistent with the essence of pantsdrunk. The difference between pantsdrunk and partying is the front door, and we will do our best to keep it shut.

## Reflections on pantsdrunk

"For me, pantsdrunk means being free from time pressures; it means perfect peace and relaxation. I start a pantsdrunk day by going to the gym and the sauna. On the way home, I stop by the store for some food and a bottle of wine. Who knows, I might buy two. Back home, I read or listen to Bellini's Norma while sipping wine diluted with water. I cook. I don't pick up the phone or answer text messages. I don't check social media. I disconnect from everything.

"After eating, I read and drink at a leisurely pace until the alcohol starts to take effect. Then I listen to music, which always means opera. Later I'll watch a DVD. For me, the best pantsdrunk movies are Bullitt and Notting Hill. I might jump up from the couch, shout instructions at the characters, and sway along with the plot. The prevailing state of mind is tranquil, observant, and wholly relaxed. A pantsdrunk day is supposed to be endless and unbounded."

— Woman, 60, open-plan office worker

# Statistics Say

*Finland is the most stable country in the world.*

*Finland is the safest country in the world.*

*Finland ranks at the top of the list in international comparisons of well-being.*

*Finns have the most personal freedom in the world.*

*Finns have the best education system in the world.*

Statistics Finland, a national agency founded in 1865, produces the vast majority of Finland's official statistics. Based on them, hundred-year-old Finland is doing pretty well.

When Finland declared independence in 1917, it was a poor, agrarian country with a GDP barely grazing the global average. Life expectancy was low and child mortality high. In a hundred years, Finland has become a post-industrial information society and the third-most prosperous country in the world.

What more convincing evidence of pantsdrunk's positive impact on societal development do you need?

# Alongside Norway and Sweden, Finland Ranks As One of the World's Three Freest Countries

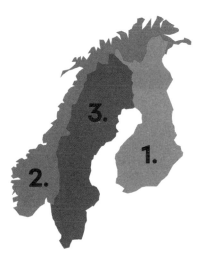

1. Finland
2. Norway
3. Sweden
4. Canada
5. Netherlands
6. Australia
7. Luxembourg
8. New Zealand
9. Uruguay
10. Barbados

*Source: Freedom House*

# What Makes for Successful Pantsdrunk?

**Timing**
When the day's work is done.

**Conscience**
"Cleanish" is good enough, no need for it to sparkle.

**Dress**
Underwear (also: sweats, pajamas, or so-called loungewear).

**Enclosed space**
Indoors is best. Restless souls may need to turn the deadbolt.

**Temperature**
Optimal indoor climate facilitates room-temperature lounging in one's skivvies.

**Alcohol**
According to one's needs and abilities. Getting wasted is NOT the goal.

**Wool socks**
The crowning touch on the pantsdrunk uniform.

**Sustenance**
Snacks: salty, sweet, or both. Think candy, crunchy, crispy.

**Diversionary devices**
Your connection to the outside world. You decide when to keep the channel open.

**Psychological well-being**
Wrap yourself in a warm state of pantsdrunkenness—and all is well with the world.

# 3
# The Elements of Pantsdrunk

*An individual sport. The four basic building blocks. Budget and the limits of moderation.*

Pantsdrunk is first and foremost an individual sport, and the most organic platform for it is an empty room. If family members, relatives, or friends happen to be present in the immediate vicinity, contact needs to be mutually avoided. Pantsdrunk that develops into social chit-chat is no longer pantsdrunk in its purest form. This does not mean that pantsdrunk entails an inherent aversion to the outside world. But as the self-determined occupation of time and space, it is at its deepest a meditative exercise. Finns know how to respect those who like to get pantsdrunk by giving them space to focus on their practice. Pantsdrunk is a sacred rite, like going to the sauna.

Practitioners of pantsdrunk willingly check their brains at the door. The goal is an authentic, honest, and present state of existence.

The flexibility and nondiscriminatory nature of pantsdrunk are evidenced by the modesty of the necessary equipment. Pantsdrunk does not require substantial investments; rather, it is a banner waved on behalf of a level playing field. It is a grassroots event that belongs to everyone.

The minimum requirements for building a proper pantsdrunk session are, in addition to pleasant or at least tolerable physical surroundings, an appropriate amount of alcohol, leisurewear, one diversionary device, and a blood-sugar-raising agent. Quantitative and qualitative variation is allowed—sometimes there's more alcohol and less clothing—but these are the basic building blocks.

# 1) Alcohol

What's a sufficient amount of alcohol for getting pantsdrunk? This answer is subjective, and various schools of thought exist. For traditionalists, going overboard is always better than not taking things far enough, but younger generations tend to conceive pants-

drunk as more closely resembling gauzy, French-style sipping than glum boozing. Both schools share the view that by morning, no reminder of the previous night should remain, other than perhaps a pasty feel in the mouth. Traditional symptoms of a hangover are a clear sign that pantsdrunk has gone too far and the practitioner needs to fine-tune his or her competence. More on this in the chapter "If Pantsdrunk Gets Out of Control."

The basic pantsdrunk beverage is beer or wine. The advantage of beer is its easy-to-control dosage. For some, based on experience and physical dimensions, two is too few, but six—or, OK, seven—is too much. Regularly conducting a control count of the empty cans is a handy way for practitioners to keep track of the total amount consumed. Beer also conveniently addresses the body's need for hydration, and intensifying trips to the bathroom reveal when the saturation point has been exceeded. More positives: according to a study conducted by Juho Leikas at the University of Jyväskylä, beer surpasses water at rehydrating the body after athletic exertion and contains more vital minerals—potassium, magnesium, silicon, and manganese—than sports drinks. In addition, the lingering buzz produced by beer is well suited to the laid-back nature of pants-drunk. Pantsdrunk is not about getting blitzed.

That said, the use of hard liquor is acceptable as long as the risks are acknowledged. Refraining from tossing back too many fingers requires judgment and firmness of will. In this instance as in most others, context is king: for instance, on a cold stormy night, a drop of cognac is the icing on the cake.

WINE AND SPARKLING WINE have grown to become credible challengers to beer since the 1990s. A well-balanced bubbly serves the same function as a decent lager or IPA, and expensive brands aren't necessary to set the right mood. More experienced practitioners will choose a sparkling wine or a full-bodied red, the ideal accompaniment to dark chocolate intended as evening snack. One weakness of wine is the size of the bottle, generally 750 milliliters. When ingested alone, this amount may be overpowering for, say, a petite female, and as the pantsdrunk progresses, leaving the bottle unfinished may prove difficult. Piccolo bottles, on the other hand, can be truly *piccolo*. Boxed wines entail substantial risks, as there is no reliable way of keeping an eye on the amount chugged. Wine also has a higher alcohol content than beer, so monitoring consumption over an entire evening demands both experience and willpower.

## 2) Dress

Dressing for pantsdrunk generally means undressing. Not because the situation entails any particular erotic charge per se, but because sufficiently loose underwear is comfortable by definition. The more advanced in age the practitioner, the more likely he or she is to procure underwear based on personal comfort, as the chances that anyone else will see it continually diminish.

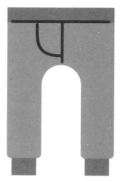

If the temperature of the room is on the cool side, the practitioner may want to contemplate complementing this basic outfit with a T-shirt or top. Another popular choice is traditional pajamas. Most men know that the comfiest forms of underwear are nonconstricting boxers and long johns that have softened with use, while the first articles of clothing women generally relieve themselves of in the context of pantsdrunk are constraining bras and nylons. The skin is meant to breathe.

In cold seasons—which in Finland means most of the year—the minimum attire may not prove sufficient. Catching a cold is a risk if some health fanatic or the individual responsible for the household finances has fiddled with the radiators or the AC. For this reason, it's always wisest to keep a pair of wool socks within arm's reach. They ensure the proper circulation in the extremities more pleasantly than sweatpants and have the added advantage of fitting into a small space.

## 3) Diversionary Devices

After intense physical exertion, it takes no more than a few minutes for the athlete's breathing to steady. The same applies to human ability to recover after a spike in stress. Sometimes a long day demands a quiet moment on the couch accompanied by deep inhalation and exhalation, but at some point the pressure eases. At this point, the pantsdrunk practitioner emerges from his or her resuscitory moment and wonders: what next? Social beings may start craving the company of other members of the same species or other external stimuli.

This is where the diversionary device comes in.

Do not let the term "device" fool you. A device may well be so-called "old school": a musical instrument, a yo-yo, a mail-order catalog from the 1970s, a book, knitting needles, nail clippers, a cheese grater, or a dartboard (not recommended). However, the recuperating individual may find such diversions overly simple and slow-tempo. As the stress dissipates and pantsdrunk progresses, the need for stimuli or bidirectional communication grows.

Music offers a foolproof way of throwing one's self into the moment. The source of this music can range from over-played vinyl from the '70s, TDK cassettes from the '80s, or CDs from the '90s to the streaming services of the new millennium—it makes no difference, as long as they produce the desired sound waves.

Of course the assumption these days is that everyone has a laptop or at least a television within arm's reach. A television in particular offers such an abundance of material of an engrossing, bracing, or even shocking nature that an individual clambering out of their emotional isolation tank will not easily find themselves bored.

Any device equipped with a Wi-Fi connection offers access to the wondrous world of the internet, where the pantsdrunk person can search for cat videos, watch the best scenes from favorite films, scour entertainment sites for important information, shop online (not unilaterally recommended), contribute to discussion forums (pseudonym recommended), or probe the depths of any topic of personal interest.

If desired, pantsdrunk also allows for the exchange of ideas or conversing, and the preferred medium for this is the internet, social media in particular. The most felicitous devices for such exchanges are mobile phones and tablets, which, unlike laptops, don't tire the wrists or heat up unpleasantly against the knees. A phone call can rapidly reveal the pantsdrunk person's not fully accountable state, but a written message, even with errors, can serve as a top-notch medium for communication.

## 4) Salty and Sweet: Maintaining Energy Levels

Pantsdrunk aims at rapid reaching of Zen, urgent repair of the psyche, and comprehensive relaxation through the proper surroundings and accoutrements. When pampering yourself, physical sustenance is also critical. No one wants their blood sugar to drop to the low end of the scale, because it's just no fun.

When pantsdrunk, normally unpermitted liberties

can be taken, which increases the euphoria inherent in a positive break from the routine. We all know how vital a balanced diet is for the health of the individual and the environment; the fuels that power the body's engine—carbohydrates, proteins, fats, minerals, and vitamins—are vital, literally so. But for the pantsdrunk, the rules can be relaxed and the food pyramid tweaked.

Because pantsdrunk isn't and should never become an everyday activity, items of questionable nutritional value can be integrated into sessions for the simple reason that doing so is possible. Pantsdrunk aims for maximizing the practitioner's state of well-being. This doesn't necessarily mean overeating or falling into a carbohydrate-induced coma, but as the practitioner's stress eases, he or she can give in to sinful culinary pleasures as the evening progresses. We are not talking about molecular gastronomy here. Optimal foods for pantsdrunk are run-of-the-mill sweets, delivered pizza, tacos, or your favorite junk food from the corner store, salami slices, olives, chocolate—in short, anything you really have a hankering for.

We'll be examining these basic elements of pantsdrunk in greater depth in the chapters to come. Don't move from that couch!

# Finns Prefer to Drink Alcohol in Their Homes or Yards

(2016)

**57%**

Own home or yard

**10%**

Someone else's home or yard

**10%**

Cabin or leisure-time residence

**17%**

Licensed establishment

**3%**

Other space for gathering/celebration

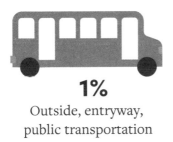

**1%**

Outside, entryway, public transportation

**2%**

Elsewhere

*Source: Finland's National Institute for Health and Welfare*

# 4
# Social Media

*On social media, no one can hear if you're pants drunk—although some might figure it out. Virtual face-saves. So many options for making a fool of yourself—pick your poison.*

Social media lends a modern, piquant zest to pantsdrunk. When watching television, listening to music, or reading a book, pantsdrunk remains a private experience, but interaction with others cracks the veil between one's self and the outside world. Depending on the conditions, the individual, and the position of the moon, this experience can be therapeutic, traumatic, or—at its finest—both.

The lowest-threshold social media is exchanging

text messages one-on-one. This form of communication provides cover and can conceal the conversationalist's psychophysical state to a surprising degree. But remember, while goofy or vulgar texting with a good friend can be hilarious, texting with employers, exes, or mothers is best avoided when pantsdrunk.

There's no way to make a fool of yourself with confidantes. They permit imperfection, tactlessness, and hyperbole. Witty, freely associative, and meandering conversations are the spice of a good pantsdrunk session.

Nor does the discussion need to remain one-on-one. Confidential conversations (meaning those in which nonparticipants are analyzed) are best engaged in closed groups, but if the topic is free and the ensuing back-and-forth feels brilliant, there's no call to restrain your verbal ingenuity.

Closed conversations and those that take place on Facebook walls are the most natural terrain for those who are pantsdrunk. Instagram and Twitter often demand concentration or even exertion, which is not conducive to the spirit of the evening. As is generally acknowledged, condensed, rapid-fire Twitter can lead nations to the brink of war, let alone trash interpersonal relationships. And Instagram demands a visual eye that's not necessarily at its keenest as midnight approaches under less-than-sober conditions.

Livestreaming, above all Periscope, is a definite no-no when pantsdrunk. Reviewing your confused mumblings after the fact is rarely a triumphal experience, regardless of how you felt at the moment of recording.

PANTSDRUNK AIMS at relaxation and complete liberation from achievement; hence the importance of striving for the golden mean with social media. Browsing and liking are safe options. If you don't have the self-control to stay mum all evening, there's no reason you can't engage with others, but it's important to remember that current technology can preserve messages for a surprisingly long time. Screen-captures are also frustratingly easy to take these days.

Based on longitudinal studies conducted at the Norra Haga Party Central Institute, we have come to the conclusion that, despite the existence of a few tricks, providing comprehensive guidelines to engaging in social media while pantsdrunk is impossible. The person-

ality traits of the pantsdrunk person play a particularly critical role. An inherent sensitivity to context is useful and can be honed and improved through experience. Note, however, that as pantsdrunk is not suitable as a nightly ritual, this means years or decades of practice. But eventually the practitioner will find his or her own rhythm through trial and error.

Blunders on social media must simply be accepted: they're part of life. On the positive side, they facilitate the joy of seeking and discovery and serve as learning opportunities. Pantsdrunk can get out of hand on social media once, twice, or ten times, but one must maintain faith that minding one's manners is a reachable goal. In this matter, patience and close contacts are necessary.

IN TERMS OF RAISING ONE'S personal profile, mixing pantsdrunk and social media has its advantages. When

# Social Media + Pantsdrunk Hierarchy of Needs

**SOCIAL MEDIA VICTORY**
(the evening's most compelling update and biggest surge of likes,
clever one-liners on other people's walls, community esteem)

**SOCIAL MEDIA CHANNELS**
like Facebook, Instagram, and Twitter
(facilitate bidirectional communication and participation)

**ONE OR MORE PRIMARY DEVICES**
that allow for an unbroken stream of stimuli
(books or magazines, Spotify, television stations, Netflix, YouTube)

**FREE WI-FI**
(a 4G connection is also acceptable, 3G in a
pinch; sufficient battery charge; electrical outlets)

**A WARM, ENCLOSED SPACE**
(protection against rain, sleet, and snow;
sufficient oxygen; food and beverage logistics)

*Source: Abraham Maslow and the Norra Haga Party Central Institute*

pantsdrunk, the practitioner is liberated enough to let loose, but generally keeps it together enough to come off to his or her advantage.

For instance, no one on Facebook really knows your perceptive analysis of Pierre Bourdieu is being copy-pasted from Wikipedia while you're farting in your grossest pair of sweats. Breaks in your writing may be interpreted as profound artistic pauses, when in reality you're slurping your boxed wine straight from the tap (not recommended).

It's possible to be charming, tactful, witty, perceptive, empathetic, intellectual, and folksy because you are concentrating on being that and nothing else. No one knows that at the same time you're scratching yourself in curious places and picking your nose—presumably with the same finger(s).

The best thing about using social media while buzzed is the magic circle of sociability it draws around friends, acquaintances, and semi-acquaintances. And yet pantsdrunk is not the right state for venturing forth and conquering completely virgin territory. The healthy, stable pantsdrunk person firmly avoids discussions and forums that inflame passions, unless that happens to be his or her forte.

## Reflections on pantsdrunk

"I get really extroverted when I'm drunk—and that goes for when I'm pantsdrunk, too. I might end up drinking at home because the bar is too far away, it's cold outside, or I don't have the energy to throw on a pair of jeans. But after a couple of glasses, I feel like chatting and I've drunk-called millions of people. These days I only keep my dad's, mom's, and brother's numbers in my phone. My friends don't answer anymore anyway. But my Facebook Messenger is on fire, of course, and the next day I'm inevitably ashamed to find a dozen new messages in my inbox. Usually I have to toss back a couple of glasses of wine before I have the guts to check who I've messaged and what sort of embarrassing drivel I've vomited."

— **Woman, 44, graphic designer**

# 5
# Etymology

*A new word for an old phenomenon. The generation gap in attitudes.*

Although the concept of pantsdrunk has been around for ages, as a term it's relatively young. *Kalsarikänni* does not appear among the eight million words in the dialect archives of the Institute for the Languages of Finland. Nor is the answer of its origins to be found in Heikki and Marjatta Paunonen's prize-winning compilation of Helsinki slang from the beginning of the 1900s to the 1990s, *Tsennaaks Stadii, bonjaaks slangii* (2000).

Riitta Eronen from the aforementioned Institute specializes in Finnish neologisms. One of her many tasks entails choosing words for the Institute's database of contemporary Finnish. Once a year, the Institute publishes its collection of neologisms, which inevitably arouses significant interest in the media and among the general public as a whole.

"*Kalsarikänni*, or pantsdrunk, did not appear in our database until the 2000s. The term has demonstrated vitality, however, as it was inducted into the online version of our dictionary in 2014," Eronen explains.

The word *kalsarikänni* appeared in printed form on a few individual occasions in the 1990s without proper contextualization, gradually gaining popularity on online forums in the early years of the new millennium. According to the Institute's archives, one of the oldest literary mentions was in an interview published in the September 2005 issue of the weekend supplement to *Helsingin Sanomat*, Finland's largest daily newspaper.

In the interview, the authors of a tragicomedy about women's alcohol use were asked when they had last been drunk themselves.

One of the interviewees was the scriptwriter Miira Karhula, who responded to the question thus: "Three weeks ago my husband and

I got pantsdrunk. This is rare, be-cause we have two small children. We were having a little reunion celebration, since my husband had been gone for a long time on business."

And where did Karhula hear the term the first time herself?

"I'd heard the word *kalsarikänni* years before and gathered it referred to a man drinking alone at home. But I found it amusing that it also perfectly described the way my husband and I spent the occasional evening. In the interview, I used the term ironically: we were supposed to spend a night on the town, but ended up pantsdrunk instead."

In 2005, Karhula was a young mother. She and her spouse had moved from Helsinki's lively Kallio neighborhood to an old house in northern Helsinki, and her free time was filled with diaper-changing and remodeling.

"We always talked about how we wanted to get downtown to eat and catch a movie, but when the kids were finally with their grandparents for the night, we were so exhausted that we'd usually just pick up some wine and watch a series on DVD. At that time it might

have been *Deadwood*, which we binge-watched. We would also drink substantially more wine than intended and end up literally pantsdrunk. Those were great evenings," Karhula says.

Riitta Eronen confirms that *kalsarikänni* was in use prior to 2005: "I heard the word for the first time in the early 1990s, when a friend of my boys, who were born in 1975 and 1978, used it in a context implying the behavior of a loser. Now those forty-year-old boys tell me they use the term ironically. *Kalsarikänni* was a jarring word and that's why it stuck with me.

"Different generations view the world differently. Here at the Institute, younger colleagues consider pantsdrunk neutral or even positive, whereas older ones see it as indicative of a sad, lonely life. But language changes: the stylistic tone of words used in spoken language may shift from slang to standard or from humorous to neutral in speakers' sensibilities. A word can take on new nuances and meanings."

# Sleepwalking While Pantsdrunk

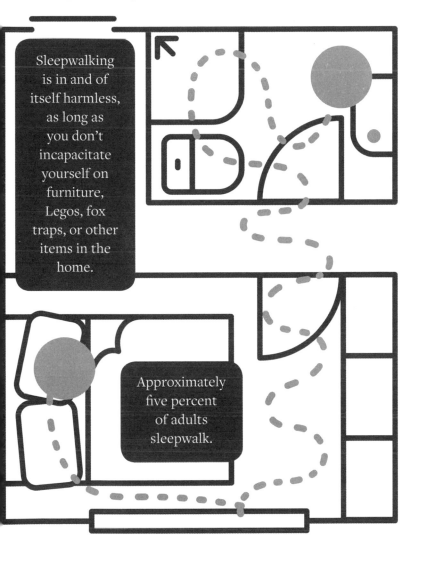

Sleepwalking is in and of itself harmless, as long as you don't incapacitate yourself on furniture, Legos, fox traps, or other items in the home.

Approximately five percent of adults sleepwalk.

# 6
# Music and Pantsdrunk— a Happy Union

*Organized noise is a message and an interpreter of mood.*

On a general level, it's worth remembering that alcohol and music is an unbeatable combination—the effervescent essence of pantsdrunk's sweet nectar! Produced in every culture that has ever existed, music can be compared to spoken language in many ways. It is a simple way of sending messages (Radiohead: "No Surprises"), expressing emotions (Lily Allen: "F*** You"), proclaim-

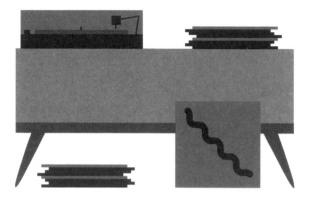

ing a manifesto (AC/DC: "Highway to Hell"), or just saying how you happen to be feeling at a particular moment (Napoleon XIV: "They're Coming to Take me Away, Ha-Haaa!").

If humans have a fondness for music in general, why on earth would pantsdrunk be an exception? Music takes us by the hand and leads us where we want to go, and occasionally to places we would prefer not to venture. Familiar songs have a tendency to reinforce our dominant emotional state, but the perceptive pantsdrunk practitioner knows the right moment to switch from melancholy murmuring to a peppier beat. It's a win-win!

One of the best aspects of pantsdrunk is controlling your own playlist. When grandpa's not around, no one has to suffer through an old hippie's yawn-inducing King Crimson/Neil Young/Gentle Giant obsessions. The absence of the younger generation ensures that Skrillex or EDM won't be thundering through the house! And yet when you're alone you're free to play all these voluntarily and at full volume, as you see fit.

Those fortunate enough to play an instrument can provide the evening's soundtrack themselves. This might not mean more than strumming a few E chords over and over again on the guitar, but hey, how cool is that?

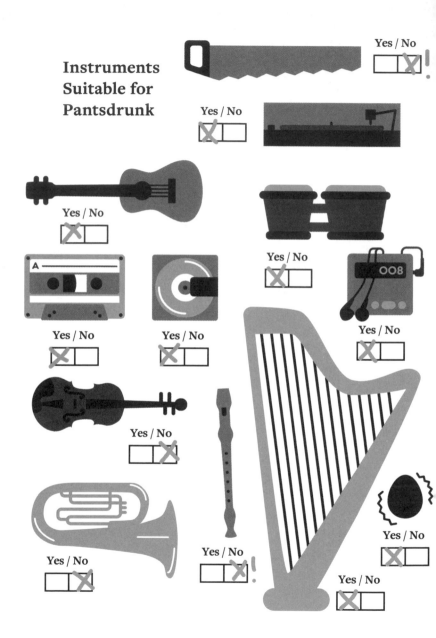

## Reflections on pantsdrunk

*"I moved into my current place in 2014, but I also lived here for a few weeks in the summer of '96. The person living here at the time was on vacation and let me stay in his place while I was here on an assignment. He had a nice collection of vinyl, and whenever work and social obligations allowed, I'd pick up a few beers from the convenience store and sit down at the stereo. My go-to was Bruce Springsteen's album* Tunnel of Love. *Nowadays I love getting some bagged beer and listening to 'Tougher Than the Rest' on my own sound system. The first beer takes me back twenty-one years; add a little cognac or vodka and the time travel continues even further."*

— **Man, 58, foreign correspondent**

# Tune Your Air Guitars

Singing and playing are signs of a healthy human—if nothing else, then silently, in front of the mirror, clutching an imaginary guitar. Pantsdrunk's physical exertions take on added swagger when you allow yourself to become a rock star for the evening. Below, the Norra Haga Party Central Institute's Sonic Vibration Department's favorites for air-thrashing, categorized by instrument.

## Air Guitar

- »   Blur: "Song 2"
- »   Ramones: "Blitzkrieg Bop"
- »   Hurriganes: "Mister X"
- »   Joan Jett & the Blackhearts: "I Love Rock 'n' Roll"
- »   Led Zeppelin: "When the Levee Breaks"

## Air Drums

» Jimi Hendrix Experience: "Manic Depression"

» Jeanette: "Porque Te Vas"

» Incredible Bongo Band: "Apache"

» Ramones: "Blitzkrieg Bop"

» Dave Brubeck Quartet: "Take Five"

## Air Bass

» The Killers: "Somebody Told Me"

» The Stranglers: "Walk on By"

» New Order: "The Perfect Kiss"

» Ramones: "Blitzkrieg Bop"

» Haloo Helsinki!: "Beibi"

## Air Microphone

» Celine Dion: "All by Myself"

» Ramones: "Blitzkrieg Bop"

» The Cure: "Plainsong"

» Nylon Beat: "Viimeinen"

» Magenta Skycode: "Kipling"

## Air Tambourine

» Blondie: "Denis"

» The Lemon Pipers: "My Green Tambourine"

» Kauko Röyhkä ja Narttu: "Sukellan taivaalle"

» Oasis: "Wonderwall"

» The Velvet Underground: "I'll Be Your Mirror"

## Reflections on pantsdrunk

"*I was living in Kulosaari and it was too far to the bars, so I'd drink at home in my underwear. I'd come up with songs I thought were fantastic and dream that I'd live off the royalties for the rest of my life. A couple times I performed them using a hairbrush as a mic, but usually I'd belt them right into Photobooth on my laptop. Oddly enough, I'd sing with my back to the screen—out of shame, I suppose. The next morning I wouldn't have the nerve to watch my performances. A couple of months ago I binge-watched these 'hits' that I almost sent to a famous producer. It was horrifying. Shitty lyrics, zero melody, cringe-inducing bleating, and me moved by my virtuosity as a songwriter.*"

— **Woman, 44, graphic designer**

# 7
# Pantsdrunk
# in Pop Culture

*Hollywood misrepresentations. Icons: Bridget Jones and the Dude.*

The deepest essence of pantsdrunk has not been comprehended correctly in all contexts. One indication of this is the fact that pantsdrunk and the activities it entails have been painted in extremely one-dimensional tones in mainstream movies. When a movie portrays an innocent individual enjoying a drink alone in their underwear, the impression is often comical, seedy, or pathetic—none of which are, of course, proper reflections of pantsdrunk.

In Hollywood movies in particular, drinking alcohol at home alone has been chronically misrepresented. Let's take four iconic pantsdrunk scenes as an example. In *The Shining* (Kubrick, 1980), Jack Torrance (Jack Nicholson) is a psychopath and a danger to his environment; in *Apocalypse Now* (Coppola, 1979), Benjamin L. Willard (Martin Sheen) is destructive to himself and his hotel room; in *Casablanca* (Curtiz, 1942), Rick Blaine (Humphrey Bogart) wallows in self-pity; and in *E.T. the Extra-Terrestrial* (Spielberg, 1982), the main character (as himself) tipples in the living room like a creature from another planet.

There are, however, exceptions in which the empowering element of pantsdrunk has been internalized correctly. One of the most uplifting performances can be seen during the opening credits of *Bridget Jones's Diary*

(Maguire, 2001), when Bridget Jones (Renée Zellweger) belts out the quintessential pajama playback solo while sloshed on red wine. Eric Carmen's "All by Myself" as interpreted by Jamie O'Neal blares and, boy, does Jones throw herself into

it, down to the drum solos. The perfor-
mance is a disarming medley of pathos,
self-pity, humor, and bad habits.

Pantsdrunk is seen more frequently
in television series. Perhaps the current
golden age of television drama allows
more daring exploration of those turning
points that take the individual forward
and reinforce their personal decisions.
These moments are mundane and frequently take place on the couch while

watching television. The tone can be solemn and dra-
matic (*Mad Men*) or carnivalistic (*Absolutely Fabulous*).
In contrast, the drinking depicted on reality shows is
generally alcohol abuse, which is used to incite the participants into committing stupidly sensationalistic acts.
Norra Haga Party Central's Ethical Council vigorously
disapproves of this.

As is clear from the aforementioned, melodramatic
self-pity does have a critical role to play in the construction of a pantsdrunk session. Overindulgent lamenting
in a spirit of carpe diem cleanses and makes it easier
to put things into proportion. Self-pity and internal

turmoil can also lead to positive outcomes, as in Sofia Coppola's *Lost in Translation* (2003). Bob Harris and Charlotte (Bill Murray and Scarlett Johansson) exist in a disconnected state of limbo caused by jet lag and an inability to communicate with the locals. Upon finding each other (and pantsdrunk), the main characters relax and are even able to get a good night's rest.

In addition to *Bridget Jones's Diary*, there are two other films where the ethos of pantsdrunk has been correctly divined. In *Batman Returns* (Burton, 1992), Selina Kyle (Michelle Pfeiffer) slurps "milk" straight from the carton, upending her values and priorities and turning into Catwoman. The barely veiled euphemism speaks to the empowering impact of pantsdrunk.

The most accurate representation of pantsdrunk is, however, to be found in the Coen brothers' cult classic *The Big Lebowski* (1998). At 32 minutes, there's a scene where the protagonist, the Dude, is lying on the rug, listening to the 1987 Venice Beach Bowling League playoffs on his Walkman after downing White Russians. Focus, bliss, contentment!

The world has a lot to learn from the Dude.

## Reflections on pantsdrunk

*"When I was a student, I lived in a commune with five other women. We had this ritual of drinking alcohol on Sundays at the kitchen table. One evening the ambiance was especially melancholy. After tossing back some joyjuice, a few roommates and I decided to ditch the gloom and doom and make a music video. The song we picked was the Rednex 'Wish You Were Here.' Three changes of clothes and a couple of hours of filming later, we had four solid-gold minutes of mortifying prancing with a candlestick in the stairwell of our hundred-year-old building. The next day, when we were hungover, we laughed our butts off."*

— **Woman, 24, freelance journalist**

# The Top 100 Excuses for Pantsdrunk

If you never give yourself permission to kick back, you will probably never truly relax. For those who need extra motivation to allow themselves a private mini-escape, we've drafted a list of the top one hundred excuses for pantsdrunk:

1. I'm done with work for the day.

2. I have to go to work tomorrow.

3. I have the day off tomorrow.

4. It's raining.

5. It's supposed to rain tomorrow.

6. It's been raining for a week.

7. It's cold outside and warm inside.

8. There are still some potato chips at the bottom of the bag.

9. My significant other is out for the evening.

10. My significant other is home for the evening.

11. My significant other fell asleep after the evening news.

12. I don't have a significant other.

13. I've never been this old before.

14. I finished cleaning the house.

15. I've never been *this* old before.

16. I should clean the house.

17. My neighbor is vacuuming.

18. I don't have a cat.

19. I found the cat!

20. The kid next door is bawling.

21. The kids are with grandma and grandpa.

22. The kids aren't with grandma and grandpa.

23. I'm supposed to bake for the bake sale.

24. I finished baking for the bake sale!

25. I finished washing the laundry.

26. I should sort the laundry.

27. I finished putting away the laundry.

28. I should clean the closets.

29. I went through the closet and pulled out clothes to sell at the flea market.

30. I should look for things to sell at the flea market.

31. I should clean my inbox.

32. I cleaned my inbox!

33. I should get rid of the files I don't need anymore.

34. I'm about to check what's in that Ikea bag gathering dust in the corner.

35. Notes from college! How is this possible?

36. I really have to do something about those CDs.

37. I'll keep the CDs for now and come back to them later.

38. I'll make a to-do list in a second.

39. Item one: make a to-do list.

40. I'm so tired.

41. I alphabetized the bookshelf.

42. I should alphabetize the bookshelf.

43. I should alphabetize the spice rack.

44. I should dust.

45. I finished that PowerPoint for tomorrow.

46. I need to do that PowerPoint for tomorrow.

47. I should draft the strategic main points.

48. I need to send those emails.

49. There's half a bottle left.

50. We have red wine?

51. There was still a little whisky left.

52. There were still a few beers left.

53. *The Voice* is on tonight.

54. Tomorrow's Saturday.

55. Tomorrow's Sunday.

56. Tomorrow's Monday.

57. Tomorrow's Tuesday.

58. Tomorrow's Wednesday.

59. Tomorrow's Thursday.

60. Tomorrow's Friday.

61. I should do something about those old electronics that don't work anymore.

62. Hey, this is an original Nokia 3310.

63. The world's first mobile phone call was made in Finland in 1991.

64. I wonder what they talked about?

65. Bring back some milk, bananas, and tomatoes from the store.

66. If systems A and C and systems B and C are in thermodynamic equilibrium, then A and B are also in equilibrium.

67. I could use a little equilibrium.

68. I'm in perfect equilibrium.

69. It's humanly impossible to lick your elbow.

70. It's true, I can't do it.

71. The Greek national anthem has 158 verses.

72. The universe is endless.

73. The Greek national anthem eventually ends.

74. I think there's one more of those exotic imported beers left.

75. I'm going to start living a healthier life tomorrow.

76. I'm going to start living a healthier life next month.

77. I should go to the gym or the pool.

78. Giraffes can't swim.

79. Giraffes are still slim and athletic.

80. Giraffe vs. Human: 1–0.

81. On the other hand: who cares?

82. Finns drink more coffee per capita than any other nation in the world.

83. The world championships of wife-carrying have been held in Sonkajärvi, Finland, since 1992.

84. The Linux operating system is a Finnish invention.

85. Finns have the most heavy metal bands per capita of any country in the world.

86. The Helsinki subway system is the northernmost in the world.

87. Finland has 187,888 lakes.

88. There's not a single public pay phone left in Finland.

89. Finland has about 3.3 million saunas and 5.5 million inhabitants.

90. Three-quarters of Finland's land area is covered by forest.

91. The average speed of a sneeze is 100 mph.

92. *Guinness World Records* is the number-one book stolen from libraries.

93. Fanta was invented in Nazi Germany.

94. A kernel of corn consists primarily of starch.

95. You drive on the right side on London's Savoy Court Road.

96. The average length of line a pencil can draw is 35 miles.

97. Anne Frank and Frank Gehry were born in the same year.

98. It's humanly impossible to sneeze with your eyes open.

99. $E=mc^2$.

100. There's always a reason.

# 8
# Moving Pictures

*It's not only what you watch, but when. Make discoveries on odd channels. The icing on the cake: LOLcats.*

We have already reviewed why a television or a screen makes for a superb supplement to pantsdrunk. But what's worth watching while getting pantsdrunk? The basis of the following report is the most recent research from the Norra Haga Party Central Moving Pictures Research Department. Preliminary results indicate that the oeuvre of Andrei Tarkovski is not suitable for pantsdrunk—well, really under any conditions.

As with music, the selection of the appropriate moving picture depends on the practitioner's level and the shifting circumstances and moods of the evening. Fortunately, contemporary technology facilitates the watching of just about anything just about anywhere.

## Movies

Starting the evening off with dramas that touch on major themes and melancholy depictions of interpersonal relationships is not recommended, but such films are perfect for easing the transition to a boozy slumber at the end of the night. Another rule of thumb to remember is that, when pantsdrunk, it's better to watch movies where following the plot or chain of events demands little in the way of concentration. These include 1) old favorites 2) crazy comedies 3) mindless action and sci-fi blockbusters.

## Television

For many practitioners of pantsdrunk, television offers the most familiar form of white noise. Particularly in locations other than the home, the chatty murmur of a television generates an easygoing ambiance, even when muted. The fact that the flicker of a television screen is so agreeable may be instinctual, so closely does it mimic a bonfire's glow. You won't find a finer form of background  noise for, say, engaging in social media.

One unavoidable fact is that the linear nature of television dictates the agenda for the would-be escapist. The broadcasters broadcast, you watch. And yet for the open-minded, this can open the door to novelty. The second-rate channel selection of hotels in particular can prod those who get pantsdrunk into areas they wouldn't normally touch with a ten-foot pole. Stepping out of one's comfort zone facilitates the making of audiovisual discoveries, reconsidering one's worldview, and gaining a deeper understanding of one's fellow humans. Deep down, a bourgeois sourpuss might actually (and secretly) delight in the constant stream of reality TV churned out by lifestyle channels, but there's no need to admit this to one's cultural reference group.

There is, however, one form of television programming where linearity is the *raison d'être*: sports. Who'd be crazy enough to, say, watch the final match of the world championships of ice hockey months after they were shown on some on-demand service? A sporting event must be broadcast down to the same fraction of a second everywhere. This serves to keep the practitioner of pantsdrunk and spectator sports solidly anchored in real life. When watching a season-deciding match alone on the couch, you are actually participating in a national or global event, and a light buzz expedites the connection to the collective experience.

# On-Demand Services

On-demand services pamper the pantsdrunk state. Regardless of the initial mood of the evening—amoebic, perky, numb, or exuberant—those pantsdrunk are sure to find the perfect programming match on the nonlinear channels available online: comedy, sitcom, drama, action. In terms of effective time usage, shorter, thirty-minute bursts of entertainment are a plus. If one episode

## Reflections on pantsdrunk

*"At some point during any pantsdrunk session, I find myself rewinding Netflix or HBO (or a series that has ended up on my VLC player through illicit means) over and over because I've dozed off. This goes on for a little while, until I suddenly start awake on the couch at 4 AM with my laptop still on my stomach. By some mysterious power, it has never fallen to the floor. My aunt used to laugh at me when I claimed I was hot-blooded as a kid, but I actually do get pantsdrunk in nothing but my underwear."*

— **Man, 38, head of marketing and communications**

leaves you hungry for more, it's always possible to devour multiple episodes in one sitting. Best of all, bingeing of this nature is neither fattening or inebriating.

The ultimate cornucopia of the moving image is

YouTube, with its infinite supply of black-and-white documentaries on young men caught in the crossfire of cultural change as they come of age in exotic countries—not to mention staggering numbers of cat videos. The next supernova will strike before you get around to watching them all! Yes, We Can Has Cheezburgers!

# Historical Highlights from Sporting Events (Reruns)

The crowning moments of spectator sports, such as the Olympics, the FIFA World Cup, or the Tour de France, are always broadcast in real-time. This is not the most felicitous arrangement for getting pantsdrunk. There are two reasons for this. In the first place, the scheduling of sporting events rarely coincides with one's personal calendar. Furthermore, pulse-raising thrills are in subtle conflict with the pantsdrunk ethos of leisureliness and relaxation. A surprising turn of events during the final period can pump the viewer full of adrenaline and send his or her blood pressure skyrocketing, which demands its own time for recovery.

# Finland Has the Most Summer Olympic Medals per Capita

| | | | Residents per medal |
|---|---|---|---|
| 1. | Finland | 17,845 | |
| 2. | Sweden | 19,211 | |
| 3. | Hungary | 20,330 | |
| 4. | Bahamas | 27,204 | |
| 5. | Denmark | 28,765 | |
| 6. | Norway | 32,716 | |
| 7. | Bulgaria | 33,938 | |
| 8. | Jamaica | 34,690 | |
| 9. | New Zealand | 37,885 | |
| 10. | Estonia | 38,764 | |

*Source: Medals per Capita*

As with movies, there's no point taking unnecessary risks with sporting events when pantsdrunk. When you feel a compulsion to sink into the exhilarating world of professional athletics, the appropriate viewing choice is already-seen sports clips guaranteed to activate the brain's pleasure center. Once again, we recommend turning to YouTube and other video services.

## A Finn Might Watch

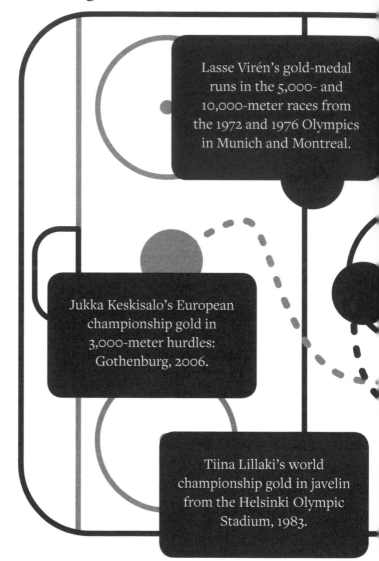

Lasse Virén's gold-medal runs in the 5,000- and 10,000-meter races from the 1972 and 1976 Olympics in Munich and Montreal.

Jukka Keskisalo's European championship gold in 3,000-meter hurdles: Gothenburg, 2006.

Tiina Lillaki's world championship gold in javelin from the Helsinki Olympic Stadium, 1983.

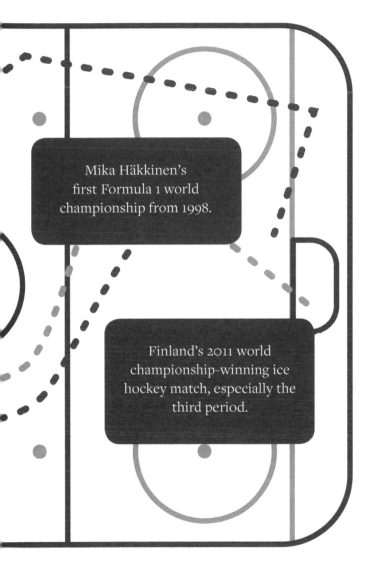

Mika Häkkinen's
first Formula 1 world
championship from 1998.

Finland's 2011 world
championship-winning ice
hockey match, especially the
third period.

# 9
# It's Official

*The Finnish government's pantsdrunk promo.*
*Finland is more than heavy metal, mobile phones,*
*and saunas. Equality for couch potatoes.*

Pantsdrunk is not just Finnish folklore or worldview; it's also official foreign policy. In December 2015, the Ministry of Foreign Affairs' Unit for Public Diplomacy launched the world's first national emojis. The original emoji selection illuminated thirty essential elements of Finnishness and were published on the thisisFINLAND (TIF) website. They were also featured in TIF's traditional advent calendar for 2015. Since then, twenty-six new emojis have been officially approved.

The first three emojis promoed heavy metal, the Nokia 3310 mobile phone, and saunas.

Jenita Cresswell, who was director of TIF at the time, remembers:

"When we were coming up for themes for the emojis, it was clear that Finnish drinking culture needed to be included. Because TIF has always constructed an unvarnished depiction of Finns and Finland, we wanted to tell about pantsdrunk. At first we considered having the man wearing long johns, because you can't get any more Finnish than that. But in the end we settled on briefs. In a tiny image, it's hard at first glance to tell that long johns are underwear; they mostly look like trousers.

"We started the pantsdrunk emojis from the man, but as pioneers in non-discrimination we wanted one for both genders. It was fun trying to think what a pantsdrunk female would look like. In the final version, she's wearing a striped pajama top and has wine in her glass, while the man is drinking beer from a pint glass. We discussed whether the woman was making an overly sophisticated impression with her wine glass and pink underwear but were pleased with the end result."

According to Cresswell, the emojis were intended for international use from the get-go, which meant the team had to think about what sort of reception they would get, as they could be perceived as the government advertising drinking. In the end, Finnishness won out. "Pantsdrunk is considered such a typical form of Finnish (drinking) culture that we wanted to tell about it, just like going naked to the sauna."

The emojis were drawn by the Brazilian graphic artist Bruno Leo Ribeiro. In addition to the core TIF languages (English, Spanish, Chinese, Russian, German, French, and Portuguese) the emoji advent calendar was published in Japanese, Arabic, Korean, Hindi, Polish, and Turkish.

"The campaign reached more than 300 million people and remains Finland's most successful promotional campaign of all time. The emojis won us almost every prize it's possible to win."

# Buying Beer

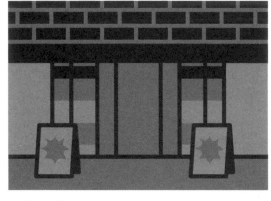

1. Choosing a purveyor

2. Reviewing the beer selection

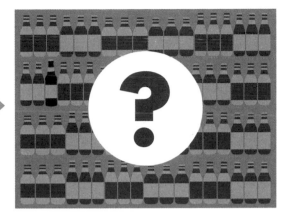

3. The decision-making process

4. Selecting the correct beer

5. Paying for your purchases

6. Enjoying your beverage

## Reflections on pantsdrunk

*"Now and again I've considered making a list of the advantages of pantsdrunk compared to drinking at a bar. I can come up with a dozen without even trying: cheaper booze, better music, you can watch TV, the bathroom's clean and you don't have to wait in line for it, you don't have to wait in line for a drink, you don't have to pay for a taxi, and you don't have to deal with idiots. That's just off the top of my head."*

— **Man, 52, unemployed**

# Accounting for Taste

The hundreds of millions of pantsdrunk practitioners around the world can't be wrong: beer is imbibed primarily for its taste. Or is it? Here is a survey of the world's bestselling ten beer brands and comments on them from Ratebeer, a website run by experts.

**3. Bud Light** (USA)
Ratebeer: overall score –/5
"One of the world's most disgusting beers." (BeerBenji)

**4. Budweiser** (USA)
Ratebeer: overall score 0/5
"If you like it, good for you. But you should go out more often or find a different crowd to hang with." (BeersNoFears)

**5. Skol** (Brazil)
Ratebeer: overall score 1/5
"This is a joke." (peponi)

**10. Coors Light** (USA)
Ratebeer: overall score 0/5
"Nice, fresh appearance. And that's about it for the positives." (d26o005p)

**9. Brahma** (Brazil)
Ratebeer: overall score 1/5
"One of the wateriest lagers I've ever tasted." (Nurmis)

**Pantsdrunk!**

**1. Snow** (China)
Ratebeer: overall score 1/5
"Tastes like water." (cagou007)

**7. Heineken** (Netherlands)
Ratebeer: overall score 4/5
"Not recommended."
(wombat23)

**2. Tsingtao** (China)
Ratebeer: overall score 3/5
"Lousy." (hrabren)

**6. Yanjing** (China)
Ratebeer: overall score 3/5
"Doesn't contain any beer."
(mansquito)

**8. Harbin** (China)
Ratebeer: overall score 3/5
"Nothing to write home about, but
at least it's drinkable." (John44)

*Sources: Bloomberg, Ratebeer.*

# Frequently Asked Questions

*Ask Norra Haga Party*
*Central anything you want. We'll reply in kind.*

## Question: I only have three hours. Do I have time to get pantsdrunk?

**Answer:** Yes. Three hours is plenty of time to ease on the psycho-emotional brakes, as long as you take steps to minimize risks and avoid the agitation caused by external stimuli. In practice, this means indulging solely in visual entertainment that has already proven beneficial, carbohydrate-rich comfort foods, and slowly relaxing, low-alcohol-content beverages like spritzers. It can take beginners years to discover their personal rhythm. Experienced practitioners know how to enhance the aforementioned elements with calming mental exercises whose foundations were laid during earlier pantsdrunk sessions.

## Question: Is it appropriate to get pantsdrunk on weeknights?

**Answer:** Pantsdrunk is not limited to any specific day of the week. Just the opposite: the restorative effect of pantsdrunk is by and large grounded in its *ex tempore* spirit. Pantsdrunk has no regard for the calendar; its potency derives from surprise. Your shackles are loosed when you least expect it. Naturally, it's important to consider your plans for the following day. If you need to depart for a business trip at 5:30 AM, it's best for the safety of everyone involved to put off the pantsdrunk by a day or two and get a good night's rest.

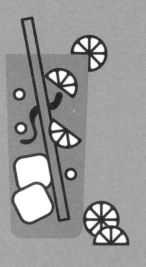

## Question: Is it OK if I feel like pantsdrunk every day?

**Answer:** No. A daily craving for calorie- and booze-fueled bacchanalia is more likely an indicator of long-term stress, depression, or a combination of both than a healthy desire to wipe the slate clean or reward yourself. If you feel pantsdrunk calling to you in the middle of the day, things clearly aren't going by the playbook. We all experience the occasional crisis, of course, and have our unique natures and personalities, but if pantsdrunk becomes routine and ceases to prompt gratifying sensations of elation, it's time to schedule a development discussion with yourself. Don't be too hard on yourself, but don't be too easy either. The importance of external peer support cannot be emphasized enough.

## Question: I prefer to get pantsdrunk with friends. Am I normal?

**Answer**: Of course. Some people are simply so extroverted that physical isolation is an impossibility. Communication is more rapid during social pantsdrunk, because body language is instantly readable. A good friend needs no more than the tiniest gesture to know to fill your wine glass or bring you a beer from the fridge. Nor is pantsdrunk as individual a sport as you might imagine. Almost without exception, it involves wasting time on social media with others in a similar state. It can be a true privilege to get pantsdrunk with a friend in the same physical space.

# 10
# Self-Pity

*Indulging in self-pity is a cleansing experience. If the emotional dead end proves to be of a more permanent nature, terminate pantsdrunk.*

Pantsdrunk is a pit stop for the soul, a quick pause for minirepairs and making sure the chassis makes it through the next stage in one piece. When necessary, it provides precision intervention in the engine block—the place where the average driver glances about five times over their lifetime. But it's critical to make a distinction between those problems that can be addressed during normal use from those that demand more invested attention.

Some negative emotional states can be repaired

through therapeutic pantsdrunk and time. Others demand longer-term internal—and perhaps external—dialogue, at which point it's important to steer clear of ethyl alcohol and avoid detours into gluttony. The ability to distinguish the appropriate form of therapy develops with life experience and the accumulation of knowledge.

To spell it out: if anxiety, depression, self-pity, insomnia, or comparable bedevilers of mental health plague at length or seem to intensify with time, pantsdrunk cannot be considered the correct solution. On the contrary, misuse of pantsdrunk will probably make things worse. For those with a history of depression or a tendency toward substance abuse, the Norra Haga Party Central Institute recommends the more developed form of pantsdrunk called *alcohol-free pantsdrunk* (more on this in the chapter "Taking It to the Next Level") and seeking the assistance of professionals.

PANTSDRUNK IS FIRST AND FOREMOST intended as a short-term therapeutic intervention to massage stress spikes into more tolerable dimensions. This Finnish form of short-term therapy is, when applied in moderation, an outstanding opportunity to bounce back from stressful situations and pressures on the job, to untangle emo-

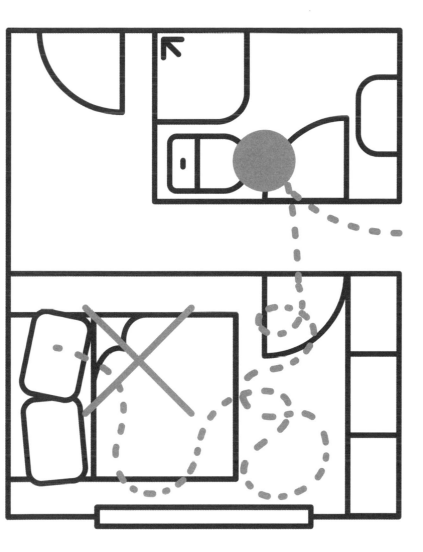

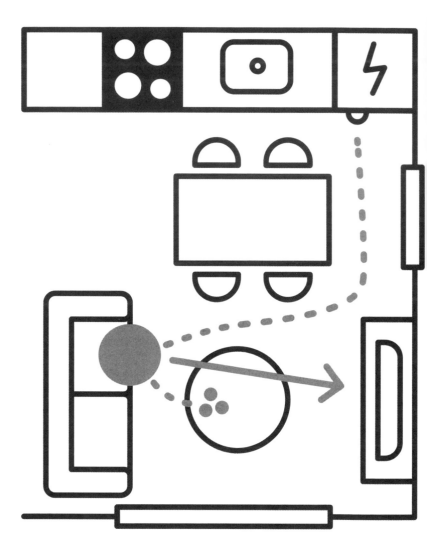

tional knots, or to serve as the impetus for their un-raveling. The experiences shared by the crime reporter (page 117) are a good example.

In a situation when, say, a relationship is ending, emotions have a tendency to rise to the surface, but society demands they remain submersed. An individual who is continuously producing agonized, teary wails in the workplace can provoke reactions of perplexity and angst among colleagues. Similarly, a party with blood-shot eyes who can't stop going on and on about their breakup may steer the agenda of a client negotiation in the wrong direction. Not to mention that the flimsy napkins provided with conference room coffee are entirely insufficient for blowing one's nose.

In Western workplaces and academia, face must be maintained whether we like it or not. Pantsdrunk is the perfect antithesis to forced maintaining of face and facades, and as such, can be an incredibly healing and liberating experience. Keeping up social appearances during a period of personal crisis is exhausting, and the resulting emotional pain might gradually harden into a psychic impasse. In this instance, pantsdrunk can serve as a dam-breaker, catalyzing critical release.

The scientific world has conducted surprisingly

little research into the healing properties of weeping. It is known that people have three types of tears. The first is basal tears, or the fluid that keeps the eye moist. The second is reflex tears stimulated by irritation of the sensory nerves in the vicinity of the face or the eyes. The third group is emotional, or crying

tears, that diverge from other classes of tears in both origin and composition. The stimulus for these psychic tears comes from the brain, and they are accompanied by the secretion of hormones. According to some researchers, crying is the body's way of ridding itself of excess hormones, hence its potential cleansing effect.

If this is the case, in stressful situations it would make sense to use little tricks to coax tears out. If psychophysical tension resists venting, try employing emotionally powerful external stimuli—such as tried-and-tested cinematic tearjerkers. When the tear ducts

open, you may as well go whole-hog and howl in misery. There there.

During controlled pantsdrunk, end-of-the-world angst can spontaneously escalate into cleansing blubbering that can be allowed to continue as long as the tears come. Wallowing in one's own feelings is a good start, and being baptized in gushing waters can be a truly cathartic experience. Perhaps even more productive is establishing contact with a trustworthy friend through a diversionary device and surveying your emotional state with them. It's best to keep unsympathetic outsiders at bay during this process—their reactions might exacerbate your angst. Resist those live feeds!

### Reflections on pantsdrunk

"I remember getting pantsdrunk during a breakup when I was twenty-five. I'd been downing a bottle of wine at a pretty rapid clip and uncharacteristically smoking at my apartment window. I was wallowing in melodramatic self-pity; mascara was running down my cheeks. The way I felt, there was no way I was going to head out to a bar. But somehow it was a rewarding and purifying experience, like pantsdrunk is at its best."

— **Woman, 35, crime reporter**

# 11
# Pantsdrunk
# on the Road

*Hotels threaten the unsuspecting traveler with boredom. Make a plan for thwarting apathy. Essentials for pantsdrunk on the road.*

Those whose hotel stays are limited to an annual vacation are blessed. For them, popping into a human night deposit box is an exotic experience every time. Someone else made the bed! The rug has been vacuumed! There aren't any toothpaste stains on the bathroom mirror!

Those for whom traveling and hotel stays are part of the job description are in a different position, however. They take up temporary residence in indistinguishable cubicles for the duration of sporting tournaments, corporate training sessions, political party conventions, book fairs, or client meetings. They are subject to death by lodging, or psycho-emotional paralysis as a result of long-term or repetitive nights away from the home. This fate can easily befall the hotel guest who is unable to come up with a pleasant way of passing the time in an unfamiliar environment, where one is lacking both one's personal belongings and the companionship of one's spouse and family.

Such situations require a strategic approach. Pantsdrunk is the perfect tool for repelling sensations of alienation, paralysis, and apathy; it allows you to bring a little piece of home with you no matter where you lay your head.

YES, SURPRISINGLY ENOUGH, pantsdrunk, the cornerstone of a happy homebodiness, also works during periods of forced exile. The key is serenity. It's critical to make time for yourself, and to do so consciously or even brazenly. We all have an inalienable right to a private moment under pressure. For this reason, those who travel frequently for work are resolute in demanding a single-occupancy hotel room of their employer.

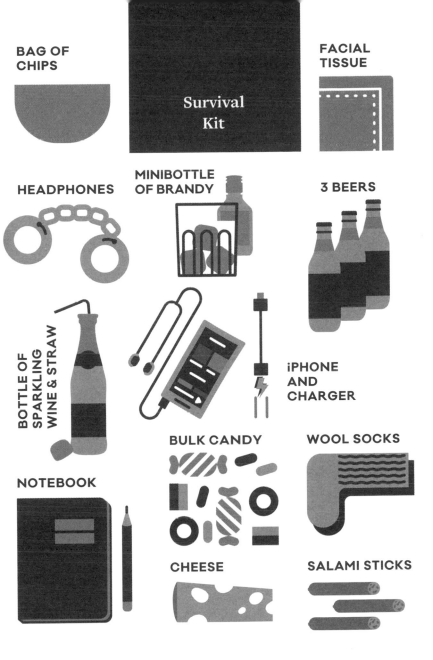

BAG OF CHIPS

Survival Kit

FACIAL TISSUE

HEADPHONES

MINIBOTTLE OF BRANDY

3 BEERS

BOTTLE OF SPARKLING WINE & STRAW

iPHONE AND CHARGER

NOTEBOOK

BULK CANDY

WOOL SOCKS

CHEESE

SALAMI STICKS

It's unusual for a conference or a seminar to take up so much time that the participant doesn't have an hour or two for an inner debriefing and battery recharging. If this threatens to happen, it's best to excuse yourself early from the last meeting of the day, claiming a splitting headache. The inherent meditativeness of pantsdrunk comes into its own when the practitioner is assured that the subsequent hours will be completely uninterrupted, without colleagues pounding on the door to, for instance, "go over tomorrow's presentation one more time."

## Helsinki Is the World's Second-Most Attractive City for Start-Ups

1. Singapore
2. Helsinki
3. San Francisco
4. Berlin
5. Stockholm
6. Tel Aviv
7. Zurich
8. Seoul
9. Hamburg
10. Toronto

*Source: Nestpick*

Successful hotel-room pantsdrunk requires that the practitioner pack a basic pantsdrunk kit. This kit includes at minimum a small selection of alcoholic beverages, a book or magazine, access to social media, snacks, and wool socks.

Those uninitiated in the theory and practice of pantsdrunk might find the wool socks puzzling, but the Thermodynamic Research Department at Norra Haga Party Central attests that those who try them once never return to their old ways. Aside from providing warmth, wool socks are incomparable at arousing the emotional associations of coziness and positivity necessary for achieving peace of mind. The origins of the use of wool socks lie in the Arctic conditions of the Nordic countries, but this innovation can be utilized in any hotel room where there's a draft or the air conditioning has been set aggressively. The ideal temperature for pantsdrunk exists in the zone where underwear and wool socks are the sole garments required for comfort. In practical terms, this means 75°–79° Fahrenheit. This is not always ecologi-

## Finland Is the Second-Best Country in the World in Which to Be a Girl

1. Sweden
2. Finland
3. Norway
4. Netherlands
5. Belgium
6. Denmark
7. Slovenia
8. Portugal
9. Switzerland
10. Italy

*Source: Save the Children Fund*

cal, but the carbon footprint of hotel-room pantsdrunk is significantly lower than that of all the flatulating cows in the world combined.

In terms of an enclosed space for achieving self-realization, a hotel room is provisional but rich in possibilities. For the price of the room, somebody pantsdrunk has redeemed a space where daring, even rash, behavior is allowed. Under such conditions, pantsdrunk can rise above the sometimes-limiting rules and conventions of the home into more multifaceted spheres: in a hotel room, no one is monitoring your doings, not even you. Temporariness and anonymity can liberate the pantsdrunk person, making it possible to find limits and move through them. No one knows if you're flinging around the clothes you stripped off, exploring the cavities of your body, or practicing basic pole-dance moves naked in front of the window. In home conditions, these activities might be frowned upon, but during hotel-room pantsdrunk, they are advisable, even compulsory.

## Reflections on pantsdrunk

*"More than once, downing three or four beers has led to me listening to my own music in a reverential stupor, watching videos I've made, and patting myself on the back in support, admiration, and rediscovered inspiration. Solitary inebriation leaves no room for self-criticism. Beer is an appropriately slow and gentle medium for ushering me into this state of nostalgic euphoria. Even red wine can be on the strong side. But at times, medium-tannin courage has a curiously beneficial effect."*

— **Man, 46, composer-musician**

# 12
# Chill!

*Drink-chilling tips for the patient and the impatient.*

As we just learned, the rapid relaxation and revivification conferred by pantsdrunk can be enjoyed elsewhere than the safe, familiar magic circle of the home. In harsh field conditions, one of the trickiest challenges for practitioners has proven to be the rapid chilling of a beer can or bottle to a drinkable temperature. Nearly every individual who has striven for DIY Zen has come across a situation in which the timing would be perfect for pantsdrunk, but the beers are vexingly room-temperature.

Alternatives for expedient beverage-chilling abound. Unfortunately, there's no method that is both fast and cost-effective. Listed are a few of the most popular tips for chilling beer, courtesy of the Norra Haga Party Central Chilling Consulting Department. Naturally, the instructions can be applied to other beverages as well, including cider and sparkling wine.

## 1) **Freezer**

Those who have a freezer and ice on hand get off easiest. However, this is generally only the case in the home, exceptionally well-equipped hotel rooms, or Airbnb accommodations. Depending on the cooling appliance, it takes 30–50 minutes to achieve a nice frost on a tall boy. Freezing a can of beer into a rock-hard brick is a giveaway that an amateur is at work; after melting, once-frozen beverages are potable but less carbonated—yuck! You can artificially boost the freezer method by wrapping the can in dampened paper toweling, but be sure that the wet paper does not drip water into the freezer. A wet paper towel will generally accelerate chilling by 10–15 minutes.

The fastest, lowest-risk method for chilling in a walk-in freezer is depositing the beers in a largish basin or bucket filled with crushed ice and cold water. This universally recognized method can be optimized by adding a fistful of salt to the ice-water mix. This method requires a little forethought, but the reward is a cold beer in as few as 2–5 minutes.

## 2) Refrigerator

An individual planning to get pantsdrunk with nothing but a fridge at his or her disposal must act quickly. Start by immediately packing the beers into the coldest spot of the appliance, generally at the rear of the lowest shelf. Reserve two bottles for special treatment. Place these under cold running water. After about fifteen minutes, the first beer will still be warm, but there's nothing to be done about this. Accept reality and enjoy. The second beer will be more tolerable.

## 3) Natural Forces

The pantsdrunk practitioner may also come across situations where the sole chilling agents are natural forces. This can happen at, for instance, a summer cabin off the electricity grid. The following chilling methods are true Finnish folk tradition, as, according to Statistics Finland, the country had a little over half a million summer cabins in 2015.

In the windsock method, a beer bottle is slipped into a dampened athletic sock, which is then hung from a tree branch. If the wind is forceful enough, the beer will be cold in half an hour. In the newspaper method, pages of newsprint are torn into strips that are then dampened

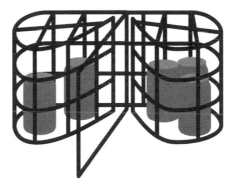

and wrapped around the bottles. The water absorbed by the paper cools the bottles. The natural water method is the best of the ecological alternatives. Load the beer into a plastic bag or a fish trap, then carefully lower the makeshift cooler into lake, river, or sea. The beverages may be cold in as little as ten minutes. The pressurized air method serves as a last resort if the craving for a cold beer proves insurmountable and you have money to burn. It requires two canisters of pressurized air, which is blown against the sides of the can. In this method, the cost per can rises to about $18.75—but hey, can you put a price on a cold beer?

# 13
# Helsinki, the World Capital of Bagged Beer

*When the temperature rises above freezing, the Finn comes alive.*

Pantsdrunk is best suited to the darkest months of the year—this is incontestable. At the time of the winter solstice, Helsinki has less than six hours of daylight per day. When this annual gloom disperses, Finns gradually awaken from their winter sleep. It's as if they're seeing the sun for the first time ever: squinting in disbelief as they survey the dazzling, light-filled landscape.

Finland has four seasons: rainy autumn, dark winter, slushy spring, and summer. The shortest of these is summer, which usually takes place during the last two weeks of July. According to the old joke, the Finnish summer is short but relatively snow-free—so when temperatures rise above freezing, the moment must be seized.

But does the Finn abandon pantsdrunk during this time? Of course not! At the onset of the thermal summer, the Finn sheds his or her winter coat to reveal a lover of the great outdoors, and pantsdrunk becomes an outdoor activity. Instead of social media, the real world becomes the arena for exchanging news and gossip. This is a surprising turn of events—but so is the light-filled Finnish summer, which can at times reach temperatures of over 59° Fahrenheit.

What's going on here? Pantsdrunk has morphed into *pussikalja*. The concept of *pussikalja* is as simple as the two words making up this delicious compound: *pussi* (plastic bag) and *kalja* (beer). How it works is this: cold beer is procured from a supermarket, packed in a plastic bag, and carried to a nearby recreational area or park for enjoyment. When the beer runs out, participants move on to the nearest drinking establishment to continue the evening.

# Finland Has the Second-Highest Number of Islands in the World

| | | |
|---|---|---|
| 1. | Sweden | 267,570 |
| 2. | Finland | 179,584 |
| 3. | Canada | 30,000 |
| 4. | Indonesia | 18,307 |
| 5. | Australia | 8,222 |
| 6. | Great Britain | 6,806 |
| 7. | Japan | 6,853 |
| 8. | Greece | 6,000 |
| 9. | Thailand | 1,430 |
| 10. | New Zealand | 600 |

Source: WorldAtlas

Finland's capital, Helsinki, has oft been described as "the white pearl of the Baltic." According to the Norra Haga Party Central Unit for International Comparisons, it is also one of the leading bagged beer cities in the world. Enjoying bagged beer on a summer's evening opens up the city in a completely new light. And there's no shortage of that light: at the summer solstice, the Helsinki sun sets for only five hours a day.

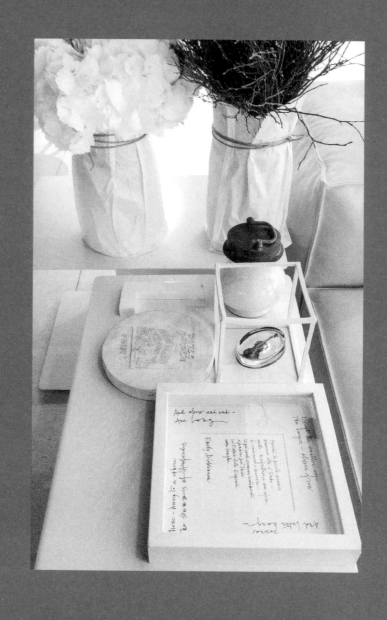

# 14
# Utilitarian Exercise

*Occupational therapy while pantsdrunk. Don't go overboard with the cleaning—chances are you won't find things when you need them.*

Despite its restorative function, pantsdrunk does not mean a complete lack of occupation. Many who get pantsdrunk satisfy themselves with lounging on the couch, which is absolutely fine. But for some, the path to the proper mood is laid by minor physical exertion, which can even be experienced as therapeutic.

According to Norra Haga Party Central's leading pantsdrunk historians, this practice has its roots in Finland's agrarian past, when there was more work to be done than there was daylight to do it in. The spread of mechanized agriculture led to the concept of leisure time, which by force of habit needed to be filled with some practical hobby or pastime. For instance, in the 1960s, when Finland was still a rural country, it was common for the female members of the family unit to engage in rug-weaving or other utilitarian activities while watching television. Knitting has retained its popularity to the present day.

On the following pages you'll find Norra Haga Party Central's tips for pantsdrunk-oriented occupational therapies. As always, restraint is advised. Urban legends tell of impetuous home-organizers who have experienced profound difficulty locating belongings after a pantsdrunk-inspired cleaning frenzy.

## Household Chores

- » Pairing unmatched black socks
- » Scraping the wax from candlesticks
- » Organizing the junk in the entryway console
- » Vacuuming
- » Replacing cracked CD cases
- » Hand-washing laundry
- » Swedish furniture: assembling, disassembling, reassembling, disassembling, etc.
- » Folding clothes
- » Knocking blackened crumbs out of the toaster

## Self-Care

» Trimming nose- and ear-hairs

» Elbow-scratching

» Applying face masks

» Squeezing blackheads

» Flossing

» Shaving legs or other body parts (Note! entails risk)

» Reading poetry written during adolescence

» Reading old diaries

» Reading old Facebook status updates

» Stomach crunches and back stretches

» Playing Candy Crush or the like on your cell phone

» Push-ups

» Listening to radio call-in shows

## Ewww!!

- » Removing hair clumps from the shower drain
- » Scrubbing the bathroom
- » Scraping unidentifiable gunk from the kitchen floor
- » Emptying the dishwater filter
- » Rabid scouring of the garbage can
- » Cleaning the oven
- » At the cabin: sanitizing the outhouse

# 15
# The Midnight Chef

*Little eats and big drinks. Highlights from the*
*Norra Haga Party Central sustenance survey.*

Credible empirical evidence confounds pooh-poohers: pantsdrunk is not the time to eat a healthy, balanced, ecologically sustainable diet. The rhythm of the evening is set with foods containing copious amounts of salt, fat, and sugar.

Why does hunger inevitably accompany pantsdrunk? Some possible explanations:

According to one theory, since alcohol is a toxin, the body breaks it down as rapidly as possible. For this reason, the calories from alcohol do not fill the belly in the same way as the calories from food or other beverages. Secondly, the desire to eat is not simply a physical urge; the human brain associates a relaxed state and alcohol with fatty foods. And thirdly, according to studies conducted at Indiana's Purdue University, alcohol improves the flavor of salty comestibles, lowering the threshold to the consumption of junk food.

So what to do? Eat, of course! Below are the highlights from the Norra Haga Party Central's extensive public survey on preferred nibbles when pantsdrunk. The results of the open-ended questions pointed to several common traits: ease of preparation, simplicity, and improvisation.

## Hors d'Oeuvres

» Prosciutto

» Potato chips

» Cheese, fig preserves

» Sausage/sun-dried tomatoes with rye bread and olives

» Baguette, Brie/Camembert and olives

» Cocoa

- » Salami
- » Takeout sushi
- » Crisp bread
- » Pickles with honey and sour cream
- » Sandwiches

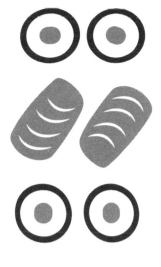

## Main Course

- » Homemade/frozen/takeout/ready-made pizza
- » Tacos
- » Supermarket sandwich jazzed up with a fried egg and oregano
- » Pasta with pesto/ham/grated cheese
- » Omelets, any filling

- » Chinese food
- » Chicken wings
- » Takeout sandwich with double jalapenos
- » Burger made from whatever you find in the fridge

## Dessert

- » Sandwich cookies
- » Ice cream
- » Chocolate
- » Bulk candy
- » Pepto-Bismol, Tums, or other antacid

# Finns Drink More Milk Per Capita than Any Other Nation in the World

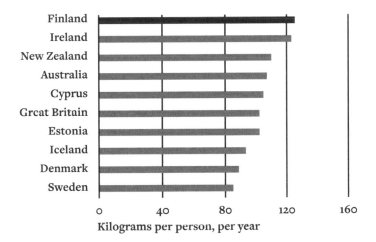

Kilograms per person, per year

*Source: Finnish Dairy Nutrition Council*

# Mixology

When selecting an alcoholic beverage for pantsdrunk, the sky's the limit. Anything goes! The aforementioned beer and wine are solid building blocks, and there's no cause to ever turn your back on them. But for those who find beer too bloating or who simply crave a change, never fear, options abound. Wine-based long drinks are a refreshing alternative that guarantee the intensity of the evening without an overly satiated sensation. For instance, a 2:1 blend of dry white wine and mineral water, or a spritzer, works regardless of circumstances. Home chefs craving more complex flavors can throw together Bloody Mary–like cocktails that also serve the function of snack.

But beware of going overboard! Pantsdrunk never involves showing off your bartending bravuras or the uptight measuring of ingredients: as with all other elements of the evening, the construction of drinks has to originate purely from personal cravings and careful tuning in to your taste buds. Say yes to relaxation and enjoyment, no to stress.

## Sangria

- » 5 oranges
- » 2 lemons
- » 1 bottle red wine
- » 1 liter lemon soda
- » ice
- » dash cinnamon (optional)

Juice three of the oranges and set the juice aside. Slice the remaining oranges and the lemons. Mix the juice and fruit with the red wine. Add the soda and ice right before serving. Garnish with a dash of cinnamon if desired. If imbibing on one's own, prepare the fruit-and-wine base in advance, chill, and add the soda and ice one glass at a time.

## Gin Rickey

- » 1½ oz gin
- » lime
- » soda water
- » simple syrup to taste
- » ice

Fill a highball with ice. Pour in the gin. Cut the limes in quarters and squeeze the juice into the glass. Toss in the juiced limes. Top off with soda water. For a little sweetness, add simple syrup, which you can prepare at home in advance by simmering 1 part water and 1 part sugar in a pot until the sugar dissolves completely. For a whisky rickey, use bourbon or rye instead of gin.

## Pimm's & Lemonade

» 1 part Pimm's No. 1

» 3 parts lemonade

» cucumbers

» oranges

» strawberries or raspberries

» fresh mint

» ice

Put ice cubes, fresh mint leaves, two slices of cucumber, and a couple of half-rounds of orange in a glass. Add halved strawberries or whole raspberries if desired. Add the desired amount of Pimm's and top off with the lemonade. Stir with a long spoon. For a larger group, prepare by the pitcher—you can always finish it yourself in a pinch.

# 16
# Three
# Sample Evenings

*Practical exercises in pantsdrunk. Take a tip or two, vary boldly!*

Previous chapters have reviewed the background and theory of pantsdrunk. Nevertheless, the practical details of a pantsdrunk session may remain unclear to some readers. How does it begin, what are the hallmarks, and why is your voice mail full of messages the next morning?

There is no need to shy from asking such questions. Pantsdrunk is tiny Finland's modest contribution to the world's psycho-spiritual heritage. Combining pants-drunk with the unique features of your local culture can produce uproarious and novel leisure-time practices.

In order to combat an overemphasis on theory, the Norra Haga Party Central Operations Team has drafted three sample evenings. Their progression provides a concrete grasp of the great variety inherent in pantsdrunk sessions, and how richly the basic theme lends itself to variation.

## Reflections on pantsdrunk

*"Buying stuff online is frustratingly tempting and easy when you're pantsdrunk. I've forbidden myself from buying clothes and shoes when I'm drunk, but for some reason buying books always seems sensible. One time a colleague marveled at a stack of books I was carrying home from the post office. I'd ordered them after a night pantsdrunk at home, and I had no idea what I'd find. They turned out to be nineteenth-century historical works from Portugal, of which I understood almost nothing thanks to my scant command of Portuguese."*

— **Woman, 35, housewife**

# Exercise Breaks

For those who do stationary work in particular, proper ergonomics lessen strain and counter the effects of poor posture that lead to maladies of the back, neck, shoulders, hands, and feet. The same applies to pantsdrunk: continuous lounging in one position does not do the body good. The couch can exert a magnetic pull, which is fine early in the evening, but at some point it's wise to heed the need for exercise breaks.

Some of the necessary exercise is provided by the logistical maintenance involved in pantsdrunk, in other words tanking on liquids and foods. Those concerned about their health do not, for instance, combine nocturnal jaunts to the fridge with bathroom trips; they maximize the number of steps taken during the evening. These and other forms of occupational therapy introduced in the chapter "Utilitarian Exercise" can raise the number of steps taken during a single evening (and night) to as high as 3,000.

Those who have a natural advantage when it comes to pantsdrunk are adults who suffer from somnambulism: unconscious walking or other activities typically done in a waking state while sleeping.

|  |  |  |
|---|---|---|
| **No-Holds-Barred** | **Low Beams On** | **Zombie** |

---
### 6 PM
---

| No-Holds-Barred | Low Beams On | Zombie |
|---|---|---|
| Stripping off clothes in the entryway | Falling facedown on the couch | Collapse in exhaustion on the entryway rug, groaning |
| Bouncing on the couch | An hour later: assuming the basic pantsdrunk position | |
| Confetti, vuvuzela, balloons | Face dimly lit by the television screen | |

---
### 8 PM
---

| No-Holds-Barred | Low Beams On | Zombie |
|---|---|---|
| Too much crazy energy to focus on the nature show | Nature programming captures the attention, wine bottle open, feeling revived as the evening news approaches | A couple of hours later: crawling onto the living room floor, groaning |
| Daring dance moves: "Bailando," "I've Got the Power," "What is Love?" | Chips or pretzels, beer, and Whatsapp | Watching nature programming a total zombie, beer opened |

|  No-Holds-Barred |  Low Beams On |  Zombie |
|---|---|---|
| **10 PM** | | |
| Hilarious texting with friends | Chuckling at cat videos and old comedy sketches on YouTube | Watching the evening news a total zombie, beer in hand |
| Preening Instagram selfies | Earbuds in, reading a book, dozing off | Complete indifference, glazed eyes |
| As midnight approaches: the engine stalls | | |
| **12 AM** | | |
| Crashing during the midnight movie, laptop on lap, glass of bubbly half-drained, unfinished status update unposted | A pizza box appears from somewhere | Watching a zombie movie, thinking it's reality TV |
| **2 AM** | | |
| | Sipping at a mug of whisky, making purchases online | |

# 17
# If Pantsdrunk Gets Out of Control

*A fine servant but a poor master. How to tell if pantsdrunk is a problem.*

Like a sword, alcohol is a double-edged instrument. Deciding when or whether to begin consuming it is one of the first big life choices a young person makes.

Why is a reflective pause called for? Some pantsdrunk practitioners may be hounded by alcoholism, a genetic tendency toward substance abuse. It's also possible to end up an alcoholic without this tendency: of heavy consumers of alcohol, ten percent end up alcoholics.

This state of affairs is muddied by the fact that intoxicants have been used throughout the known history of humankind. Archeological evidence dating back at least 10,000 years indicates the human use of psychoactive substances. Every cultural sphere has had and still has its local intoxicants. In some Arab cultures, puffing cannabis has been a tradition; in the Andes, folks have chewed the leaves of the coca plant; and in the West, the preference has been for alcohol. A contemporary twist is that intoxicants no longer remain in their native cultural spheres but travel around the world.

Intoxicants are consumed for pleasure and can also be used to numb anxiety. When you're high or tipsy, life is good and things roll along smoothly. In general, Western cultures tolerate alcohol, but the legality of other substances—particularly cannabis—depends on one's country or state of residence. There is no consistent logic to the legislation; instead, it depends on the unique cultural traits of a given society or governed area. One thing is clear, however: in the current era of prosperity, the threshold to accessing psychoactive substances is low. This demands that citizens possess solid basic information about the threats and opportunities of intoxicants.

There's no such thing as an intoxicant-free society

for the simple reason that the alcohol business generates significant income for its owners, not to mention tax revenue for the state. Prohibition was given a whirl after the First World War in several countries, including Finland and the United States, but didn't accomplish much aside from boosting organized crime and overall disregard for the law.

So the responsibilty for and freedom of enjoying alcohol are left on the individual's shoulders. If alcohol has a strong pull on you, two pieces of advice: practice makes perfect, and remember there are other ways of dealing with stress. If pantsdrunk becomes compulsive, isn't relaxing, or the next day is no fun, it's best to quit.

## Reflections on pantsdrunk

*"Hungover. A long evening followed by a slow morning. A solo brunch scraped together from last night's leftovers and the dregs of the bottles. At home all day, staring at the TV, taking catnaps, and telling myself how serene I feel."*

— **Woman, 53, museum curator**

# Activities to Avoid While Pantsdrunk

1. Sending job applications

2. Updating the Wikipedia article about you

3. Repairing or cleaning precision mechanical devices

4. Engaging in an air-clearing conversation with your ex

5. Drawing up your will

6. Dyeing your hair

7. Contacting a childhood acquaintance

8. Serving as chief operator of a nuclear power plant

9. Emailing your boss or subordinates about dealbreaking concerns

10. Trolling questionable online forums under your own name

11. Making flight or hotel reservations

12. Correcting a decades-old misunderstanding with a friend in a constructive spirit

13. Buying or selling stocks

14. Painting your fingernails

15. Testing your scuba equipment in the bathtub

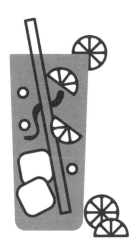

16. Advanced yoga poses

17. Formatting and partitioning your hard drive and installing Linux

18. Tattooing (yourself or others)

19. Getting a genius business idea after watching three seasons of *Breaking Bad*

20. (Even simple) electrical repairs

21. Preparing kidneys (or anything) flambé

22. Replacing the ignition coil on your chainsaw

## Reflections on pantsdrunk

*"I joined the Social Democratic Party while pantsdrunk. I read the original party platform from 1903, cried a little, and then joined. I'm still a member."*

— **Woman, 42, CEO**

# 18
# Taking It
# to the Next Level

*The mind and its control. Taking it to the next level: pantsdrunk without alcohol.*

In this book, we have covered pantsdrunk at the relevant breadth and depth. The aim has been to reveal to readers, through concrete examples and practical instructions, the primary goals of pantsdrunk: claiming your space, calming down, and recovering from stress.

Pantsdrunk is an attitude and a philosophy of life that starts from inner peace. When your mind is light and your foundation is stable, goodness is transmitted to those around you. When you love yourself, you love others, too. And achieving all this requires nothing more than comfy underwear, a moderate amount of alcohol, a few nibbles, and a diversionary device!

Pantsdrunk demands, in addition to external arrangements, the ability to process your own feelings and train the brain's control center. If the aim of pantsdrunk is simply to get drunk, you've missed the point.

## One satisfied practitioner of pantsdrunk

*"When I got divorced ten years ago, the simple notion of pantsdrunk scared me. It struck too close to the idea that a person who drinks at home alone is nothing but a lonely alcoholic. And so I spent my evenings gadding about cultural events or hosting dinners. Gradually I settled down, my self-confidence returned, and life mercifully generated an equal sign between pantsdrunk and a pleasant evening at home. This doesn't mean I never go out, and I still have people around to cook for and fuss over.*

"But I've also learned to love quiet weekend nights where I have no one but myself for company. These evenings begin in the kitchen, where I open a bottle of wine; some of it usually sloshes into whatever I'm cooking. Classical music is playing from an ad-free radio station. Then I eat and drink in front of the TV, watching a carefully selected movie or series. I might even spend some time on social media, but I've learned to avoid Friday-night outbursts. The bottle empties, my mind slows, and since I pop an ibuprofen before bed just in case, there's no hangover the next morning either."

— Woman, 58, PhD

Let's use an example to aid our reflections. Pants-drunk can also be achieved without alcohol. How is that possible, you may ask. But why wouldn't it be? If you're motivated to relax rapidly and know how to claim your space, in the end it's all the same if you're sipping on generic beer or organic apple juice (tip: you can compensate for leaving out alcohol by investing in non-alcoholic beverages of a slightly higher caliber).

When a seasoned practitioner has internalized the other relaxation methods essential to proper pantsdrunk, taking pantsdrunk to the next level is surprisingly simple. At this point, pantsdrunk is closer to mindfulness thinking than it is to the Nordic notions of *hygge* or *lagom*. A real pantsdrunk pro knows how to be his or her relaxed, authentic self regardless of the circumstances. A challenging or chaotic day swiftly takes on more tranquil tones when you remind yourself what even the sharpest suits and most flawless fashions conceal: beneath our clothes, we're all wearing underwear.

Ultimately the choice is personal. In the meantime, Norra Haga Party Central wishes you a cozy evening—pantsdrunk or not.

Cheers, or as we say in Finland: *Kippis!*

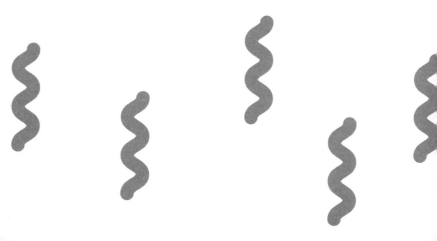

# Finland is the happiest country in the world

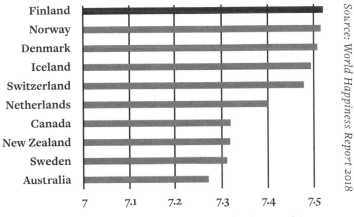

(2015-2017 Index Rankings, in thousands)

Source: World Happiness Report 2018

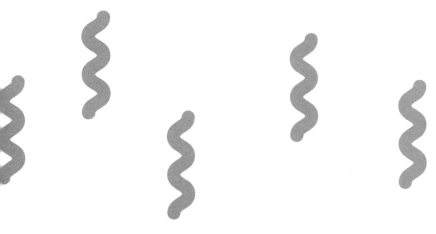

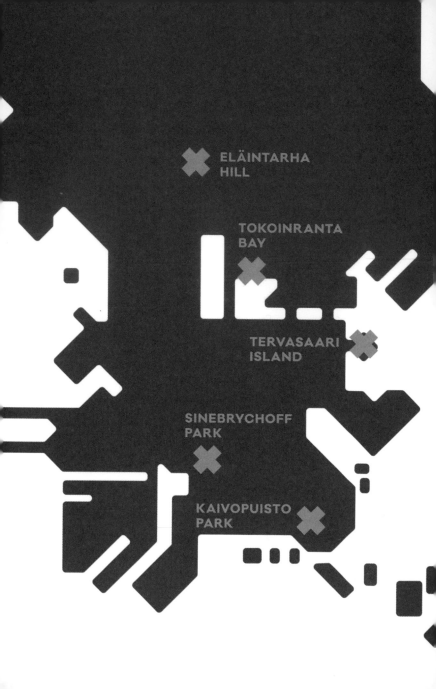

# Norra Haga Party Central's best bagged-beer venues in Helsinki

## 1 Kaivopuisto Park

A classic. This park was established at the southern tip of Helsinki in the 1830s, following the construction of a spa frequented by St. Petersburg high society. Favored by the tradition-conscious. From the rocks, a fantastic panorama across to Suomenlinna fortress and over the Gulf of Finland.

» **The night continues at: Sea Horse.**

## 2 Tervasaari Island

Multisensory exoticism. From the shores of this little island right off Kruunuhaka, vistas open up to the stages of the Flow Festival, the icebreakers parked for the summer, and the neoclassical Empire-style headquarters of the Ministry of Foreign Affairs. The cherry on top is listening to the roars of the lions from Korkeasaari Zoo.

» **The night continues at: Kolme Kruunua.**

### 3 Eläintarha Hill

Stadium concerts and sports! From the apex of the hill between the swimming stadium at the botanical gardens, you can enjoy the concerts at the Olympic Stadium for free – not to mention the soccer matches where the Finnish national team will inevitably lose.
» **The night continues at: any of the sports bars near the hockey arena.**

### 4 Sinebrychoff Park

Hang out with the locals. Sinebrychoff Park, or "Koffari" as it's affectionately known, was originally part of the Sinebrychoff brewery. A brick tower erected in the 1860s serves as an unmistakable landmark. Popular with the hipsters and others. During wintertime, it's possible to combine sledding with beer-bagging.
» **The night continues at: Salve.**

### 5 Tokoinranta Bay

Downtown Helsinki's most stunning sunsets. If the ambiance is overly picturesque, one can increase the sense of danger by seeking out the company of the local drinking professionals, for whom bagged beer is more than a way of life. Proceed with caution.

» **The night continues at: Rytmi.**

## **Bonus:** Koskipuisto Park in Tampere

For those who want to expand their horizons beyond Helsinki, we recommend driving 110 miles northward to Tampere, the largest landlocked city in Finland (and all the Nordic countries, for that matter). Spend the evening drinking bagged beer on the banks of the Tammerkoski rapids, where you'll enjoy magnificent views of the city's nineteenth-century industrial milieu.

» **The night continues at: Plevna.**

# Acknowledgments

Shepherding this book from a tantalizing suggestion by my editor Mirjam Ilvas into a physical object has been the most fun I've had in ages. The original idea was to create a modest, satirical send-up of fluffy-as-air lifestyle guides, but the topic ran away with me and morphed into an analysis of Finnish mindfulness philosophy. Since then, we've come to believe there's something special enough here to resonate on a global scale. And apologies to the Danes and Swedes for the jabs; as you know, we Finns love you!

A huge thanks to the countless folks who pitched in on this project—I couldn't remember every name if I tried. The contributions of friends, acquaintances, and

strangers have been invaluable to proving the accuracy of my working hypothesis: pantsdrunk is a phenomenon recognized and understood by all Finns in more or less the same way. Hopefully the essence of Finnish Zen has now been satisfactorily documented and instituted as part of our shared Nordic cultural heritage.

A special thanks to Mielitietty, Tytskä, Poitsu, Janita Cresswell, Taika Dahlbom, Riitta Eronen, Riku Jokinen, Miira Karhula, Teemu Leminen, Esa Lilja, Leena Pallari, Sameli Rantanen, Tuike Rantanen, Jutta Sarhimaa, Jari Sedegren, and Merja Tirinen, as well as friends, colleagues, and acquaintances from social media.

The author is the director of the Norra Haga Party Central Institute. He has spent fifty years researching the Finnish way of life.